Mike East went out to meet the world after a spell of teaching in the Sudan. His globe-trotting has taken him from the gun-running towns of the North West Frontier to bandit country in the Horn of Africa. Seeking the quieter waters of the Caribbean, Mike first wrote about Barbados, then moved on to co-author the Lascelles guide to the Bahamas. Whilst based in Britain he writes freelance articles for a variety of magazines.

Dedication

To happy times spent with Alexandra

Acknowledgements

The author would like to thank the following people who have greatly assisted in the preparation of this work: The staff off the Trinidad and Tobago Tourism Development Authority, and of the Tobago Division of Tourism; Bill Preston and Hugh Ramsey of the British High Commission; Barbara and Fred Zollna; POS-HHH especially Lorin, Peter and Roy; Susan B, Jenny B and Jenny R; Marie Dilworth; the staff of the Public Transport Service Corporation; Rod, Joan, Bar, Martin and Pam; Mike, Roy and Les; Marcella Randall; and Roger Lascelles.

Front Cover: *Pigeon Point, Tobago – one of the most idyllic beaches in the Caribbean.*

Lascelles Caribbean Guides

TRINIDAD & TOBAGO

A Traveller's Guide

Mike East

Roger Lascelles, **Cartographic and Travel Publisher**
47 York Road, Brentford, (Middx) TW8 0QP. Tel: 081 847 0935 Fax: 061 568 3886

Publication Data

Title	Trinidad and Tobago
Typeface	Phototypeset in Compugraphic Times
Photographs	Front cover photograph by the Author. Photographs on pages 32, 33, 43 and 77 courtesy of Trinidad and Tobago Tourism Development Authority. Other photographs by the Author.
Maps	Mike East
Printing	Kelso Graphics, Kelso, Scotland.
ISBN	1 872815 24 3
Edition	First edition June 1992
Publisher	Roger Lascelles 47 York Road, Brentford, Middlesex, TW8 0QP.
Copyright	Mike East

Distribution

Africa:	South Africa	Faradawn, Box 17161, Hillbrow 2038
Americas:	Canada	International Travel Maps & Books, P.O. Box 2290, Vancouver BC V6B 3W5.
	U.S.A.	Available through major booksellers with good foreign travel sections
Asia:	India	English Book Store, 17-L Connaught Circus, P.O. Box 328, New Delhi 110 001
Australasia:	Australia	Rex Publications, 15 Huntingdon Street, Crows Nest, N.S.W.
Europe:	Belgium	Brussels – Peuples et Continents
	Germany	Available through major booksellers with good foreign travel sections
	GB/Ireland	Available through all booksellers with good foreign travel sections.
	Italy	Libreria dell'Automobile, Milano
	Netherlands	Nilsson & Lamm BV, Weesp
	Denmark	Copenhagen – Arnold Busck, G.E.C.
	Finland	Helsinki – Akateeminen Kirjakauppa
	Norway	Oslo – Arne Gimnes/J.G. Tanum
	Sweden	Stockholm/Esselte, Akademi Bokhandel, Fritzes, Hedengrens.Gothenburg/Gumperts, Esselte. Lund/Gleerupska
	Switzerland	Basel/Bider: Berne/Atlas; Geneve/Artou; Lausanne/Artou: Zurich/Travel Bookshop

Contents

16 Tobago

Getting the best out of this guidebook

Accommodation

The costs of hotels are calculated in US dollars from the basic rate for the room without meals (European Plan, EP), in the winter-high season (16 December to 15 April). Top ($121 plus), high ($91-$120), middle ($61-$90), moderate ($31-$60) and budget ($30 and under). VAT at 15% should be added to these prices and sometimes a 10% service charge on top. Enquire in advance as these surcharges are not usually quoted. On average prices tend to be between 10% and 40% less in the summer-low season.

If the charge includes meals it has been noted with the following symbols:

AP = American Plan: room with three meals.

BB = Bed and Breakfast.

MAP = Modified American Plan: room, breakfast and dinner.

Places to eat

Estimated restaurant costs are based on three courses without drinks; cafes are based on the price of a 'filling' meal. The eating places are divided into sections depending on the style of food served. They are in order of recommendation.

Credit Cards

After each hotel and restaurant review, the credit cards that may be used therein are listed. Abbreviations: AMEX = American Express, MC = Mastercard, V = Visa.

Currency

At the time of going to press one Trinidad and Tobago dollar (TT$) was worth about 15 English pence, or £1 = TT$ 7. One US dollar was worth approximately TT$ 4 or TT$ 1 to the quarter.

Trinidad or Tobago?

I have tried not to say Trinidad when I mean Trinidad and Tobago as Tobagonians are rightly annoyed by this. I have either said the country's name in full or used the term 'Trinibago'.

Language

To avoid confusion between the different phraseology used in North America and Europe (e.g. gasoline/petrol or liquor/alcohol), local terms are used throughout.

Addresses

A mixture of house delivery and PO boxes is the norm, this book therefore uses both.

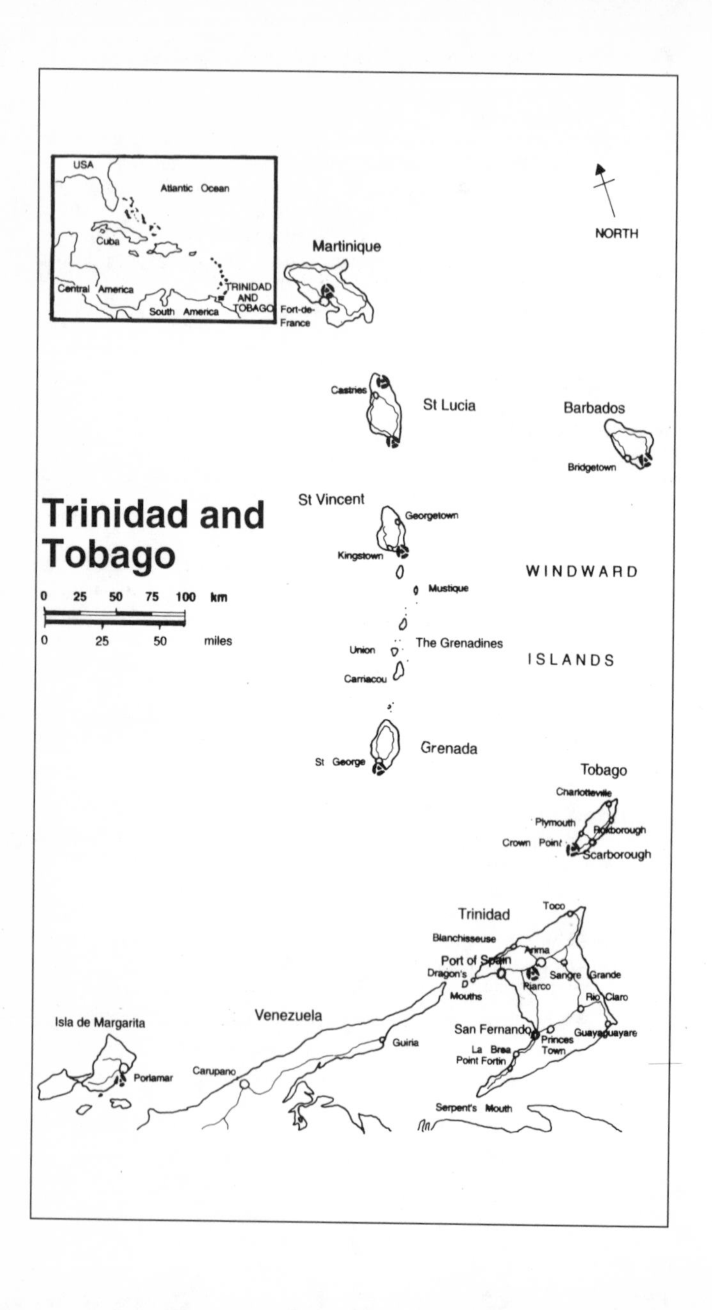

Trinidad and Tobago
0 25 50 75 100 km
0 25 50 miles
USA
Atlantic Ocean
Cuba
Central America
South America
TRINIDAD AND TOBAGO
NORTH
Martinique
Fort-de-France
Castries
St Lucia
Barbados
Bridgetown
St Vincent
Georgetown
Kingstown
WINDWARD ISLANDS
Mustique
The Grenadines
Union
Carriacou
Grenada
St George
Tobago
Charlotteville
Plymouth
Crown Point
Scarborough
Trinidad
Toco
Blanchisseuse
Arima
Port of Spain
Dragon's Mouths
Sangre Grande
Piarco
Rio Claro
San Fernando
Princes Town
Guayaguayare
La Brea
Point Fortin
Serpent's Mouth
Venezuela
Guiria
Carupano
Isla de Margarita
Porlamar

ONE

Introducing Trinidad and Tobago

If, on a cold winter's day you glance at an advert extolling the virtues of the Caribbean, there is a very good chance that the idyllic view used to spirit you away will be from Tobago. Pigeon Point, perhaps more than anywhere else captures the essence of why so many people come to the Caribbean. Its powdery white sand edged on one side by protective palms and on the other by a brilliantly turquoise sea is hard to better.

However, this is a country which has so much more to offer than its shoreline. Here you are in the most colourful and diverse nation in the Eastern Caribbean. People from every corner of the globe have made Trinidad and Tobago their home. First were the Amerindians, then Europeans from a dozen different nations, followed by Africans brought over by the abhorrent slave trade. East Indian and Chinese people came to work in the nineteenth century, followed later by settlers from the Middle East.

In some places such a racial melting pot would be a recipe for disaster but not on Trinidad and Tobago. 'Here every creed and race find an equal place' says the national anthem, and on the whole this is true. There is a warmth and positve attitude to life; grudges are forgotten not borne. The historical chips on peoples shoulders that bedevil other societies do not linger here.

A national consciousness has emerged and with it one notable peculiarity: the 'lime', or more accurately, the art of liming. When first hearing this term it is confusing. It seems to slip into so many sentences. This lime is no fruit drink but an immensely versatile verb-noun. You can go to a lime, or be liming. Whatever, in the art of hanging out with friends and having a good time, Trinidadians and Tobagonians are experts.

Carnival is a monumental party, an explosion of colour, music and dancing. But this is not spontaneous, it has been meticulously prepared from the final seconds of last year's celebration. What the

Recently one of the country's most esteemed steel bands, the Amoco Renegades, opened their panyard to the public. Now it is possible to hear pan music all year round, rather than just over Carnival.

visitor sees is the result of thousands of hours' work by thousands of Trinidadians.

It does not stop here, the calendar is packed with many other official and unofficial festivals. Whether it is Christian Easter, Hindu Divali or Moslem Hosay the people celebrate enthusiastically.

With such a rich resource of people, an exciting culinary experience awaits the visitor. Creole, Indian and Chinese cooking has been long established. This is now being mixed with new gastronomic schools of thought. Italian, Arabic and Mexican dishes have arrived.

The nation's music is world renowned. The steel, or as it's known, 'pan' band, was invented here and continues to thrive. The versatility of these groups has been shown by the recent pan-jazz and pan-classical festivals. Combine this talent with the cheeky style of the calypsonian, home grown 'soca' and classical Indian sitar, and you have a huge variety to choose from.

So which island do you choose? Both if you possibly can. Each has something the other does not and connections between the two are plentiful.

Tobago is fringed with dozens of bays, some of which you can have entirely to yourself, others with all the facilities you could wish for. The mountains, waterfalls and rainforest make interesting diversions and the choice of sporting activities is good. Tobago has an intimate ambiance, being an island of small village communities, high rise development – never!

Trinidad, and especially Port of Spain is where you will notice the cultural diversity most of all. Here the pace of life is faster, the nightlife is hectic and plentiful with lots of pubs, clubs and concerts to choose from. The combination of the rainforest-coated Northern Range and Caroni Swamp have been a mecca for naturalists long before the phrase eco-tourism was invented.

So ladies and gentlemen the choice is yours....

Trinidad and Tobago – did you know?

– The world's first oil well was drilled at La Brea, Trinidad by the Merrimac Oil Company. Seen as a crazy idea at the time – would it ever catch on???
– Trinidad was part of South America 12,000 years ago.
– 'Trinis' claim that the Savannah park in the centre of Port of Spain is the largest roundabout in the world.
– According to Trinidad folklore no home is safe from deadly female vampires called Largabless, who fly in whilst their victim sleeps.
– Tobago was chosen by Walt Disney to be the idyllic setting for the film *Swiss Family Robinson*.
– Trinidad has its own version of voodoo called shango.
– Tobago has been one of the most coveted pieces of real estate in the world. It changed hands 31 times before finally going to Britain.
– Daniel Defoe may have used a description of Tobago as the basis for Robinson Crusoe's island.
– The internationally acclaimed writer V S Naipaul grew up in central Trinidad.
– In the early twentieth century, Trinidad's famous Carnival used to be notorious for rioting and brawling.
– Trinidad was once the site of a large US miitary base.
– The only classical musical instrument invented in the twentieth century was the steel drum from Trinidad.

TWO

Before you go

When to go

The climate splits into two quite distinct periods: the dry season between December and May, and the wet from June to November. The temperatures change little through the year, averaging 28°C (82°F) during the day and 23°C (74°F) at night.

During the rainy season the mornings usually start off fine, the sky clouds over later and there is often a shower in the afternoon. Most downpours are brief, tending to be followed by another period of sunshine. You can expect eight hours of sunshine on average per day.

If you are planning to travel over the Carnival period book a long time in advance because even if you can find a room you will not necessarily get a flight.

Prices

Most hotels lower their rates over the summer and raise them during the week of Carnival. Hotel rates are a lot more reasonable than in other parts of the Caribbean.

For everyday items, Trinidad and Tobago are probably the cheapest places in the Eastern Caribbean; it is significantly cheaper than Barbados, for example. Locally made products are good value including fruits, vegetables, cakes, pies, soft drinks and beer. As toiletries are largely imported they tend to be more expensive, but the one item that should be bought back home is film for your camera.

Eating out is again very reasonable. Filling snacks can be found for one pound (US$ 1.50), whilst the most extravagant places will be little over £20 (US$ 30), per head. Some restaurants will add a 10% service charge and perhaps 15% VAT as well. Imported wines, spirits and liqueurs are pricey due to government duties.

The view of Port of Spain and the Gulf of Paria, from Fort George, sited on the hill which overlooks the capital from the north west.

Passports and visas

All visitors must bring their passports with them. A return or onward-going ticket is another requirement of entry.

The usually permitted length of stay is for two to three months except for Venezuelan visitors who are only allowed to remain for a fortnight. Visas are not required by United Kingdom, United States, European Community, Canadian or most Commonwealth citizens (except Australians and New Zealanders who do require visas). They are not necessary for citizens of Austria, Finland, Israel, Iceland, Norway, Sweden or Switzerland, either.

If you are unsure contact the nearest Trinidad and Tobago Embassy or High Commission.

Travel alternatives

Packages

A package holiday is probably the cheapest and most convenient way to visit Tobago. This will include flight, room and often the transfer from the airport. Trinidad lends itself more readily to touring, as the island's sights are more spread out than on Tobago. There are guesthouses and bed and breakfast style accommodation all over the island which can be reached in a leisurely day's travel.

Contact your nearest Trinidad and Tobago Tourism Development Authority for more information on packages or accommodation listings:

Canada:
40 Holly Street, Suite 102, Toronto, Ontario, M4S 3C3, tel. (416) 486 4470/1.
United Kingdom:
8A Hammersmith Broadway, London W6 7AL, tel. (081) 741 4466.
United States:
Suite 1508, 25 West 43rd Street, New York, NY 10036, tel. (TOLL FREE) (800) 232 0082.

Independent travelling

There is a booth at Piarco International Airport staffed by volunteers from the Bed and Breakfast Association. It is open during normal business hours and will arrange accommodation in its members' houses free of charge.

Another possible saving is to look for a discounted or 'bucket shop' ticket. Check the advertisements in a newspaper or magazine with a good travel section. Cheaper tickets certainly do exist but you have to track them down.

Tourism with a difference

As package tours and mass tourism spreads worldwide, there is now a counter movement which is steadily gaining in popularity. This is 'Intercultur', or social tourism, a new type of cultural exchange. In return for a small registration fee this organisation arranges a host person or family for visitors. Accommodation can vary widely with costs being kept to a minimum. As a guest you are expected to contribute about US$ 40 per week to household costs.

The advantages are that this type of vacation is substantially cheaper than staying in a hotel. You are able to meet people from the country you are visiting and get a deeper understanding of them. It is a chance to make new friends. Even so, normal precautions, such as travel and health insurance should still be obtained.

As yet there is no scheme in Trinidad and Tobago though the UK branch may seek to establish one in the near future. Contact Intercultur GB, c/o CRS Ltd. Political Committee, 78-102 The Broadway, Stratford, London E15 1NL (tel. 081 534 4201 ext. 271). Social Tourism was conceived by the German Young Friends of Nature: NFTG-Intercultur, Postfach 2157, Rosenstrasse 1, 4806 Werther, Germany. In North America there is the Center for Responsible Tourism, which seeks to educate people as to the effects of mass tourism: 2 Kensington Road, San Anselmo, CA 94960 (tel. 415 258 6594). Its general philosophy is similar to European Social Tourism.

Having a hassle-free stay

In Port of Spain you could face any of the dangers that exist in any large city. Ostentatious displays of wealth should be avoided. In the countryside and on Tobago the risks drop appreciably.

Macho attitudes towards women prevail in most sections of society, though there are large and increasing numbers of women represented at all levels in the workforce. Female travellers can expect a lot of attention from Trinidadian and Tobagonian males. If it's not what you are looking for, a firm 'no' is understood when the more open signs of disinterest fail.

The dress code is relaxed but not to the extent of wearing beachwear around town. During daylight hours it is safe to walk around all areas by yourself. At night it is advisable to avoid downtown Port of Spain and Laventille, and to get a taxi straight to your destination. Never cross the Savannah at night and take care walking round it after dark (see section 8 on crime and safety below).

In downtown Port of Spain at night, lock the doors of your car and use the air-conditioning rather than riding with the windows down.

Taking the children

There are no children's 'camps' or Club Med-style resorts on Trinidad or Tobago. However, the following places offer babysitting upon request:

Trinidad: Hilton, Holiday Inn, Hotel Normandie, Royal Hotel and Valley Vue Hotel.
Tobago: Arnos Vale Hotel, Blue Waters Inn, Grafton Beach Resort, Kariwak Village, Mount Irvine Bay Hotel, Palm Tree Village and Turtle Beach Hotel.

Other places may be able to arrange something if you give them sufficient time.

Travel for the disabled

Regrettably neither Trinidad nor Tobago cater specifically for handicapped visitors. In Port of Spain and Scarborough, the capital of Tobago, pavements are narrow with high steps. It is a country where you really need an able-bodied companion.

On Trinidad there are two hotels which can cater for disabled travellers. Monique's Guesthouse has a room specially designed for wheelchair access, with a wide door, grip bars and a large washroom, as well as access to either the street or the rest of the building. The Hilton has two specially designed rooms and ramps or lifts installed throughout the complex. Turtle Beach on Tobago has facilities for the handicapped.

Before you go travel, advice can be obtained from the Royal Society for Disability and Rehabilitation, 25 Mortimer Street, London W1N 8AB, tel. 071 637 5400 or the (US) Society for the Advancement of Travel for the Handicapped, 26 Court Road, Brooklyn, NY 11242, tel. 718 858 5483.

In the air, travellers can expect airlines to provide wheelchairs if given one day's notice. In the US, the Department of Transport publish *Air Transportation for Handicapped Persons*, which gives details of in-flight facilities. In the UK the Civil Aviation Authority publish a similar booklet called *Care in the Air*.

A mixed group of school children enjoy a dip in a pool on a school outing. An excellent way to cool down in the midday heat.

Taking pets

With a strict six month quarantine it is not practical to bring animals with you unless you are emigrating.

Health and vaccinations

Travel insurance

Make sure you are covered for all possible medical problems, especially the costs of any emergency treatment. The current recession means that the health service is not as well funded as it could be. Insurance should therefore cover air ambulance – if a major accident or illness occurs you may be flown either to Port of Spain or out of the country.

Do not expect the locals to drive in the same way as you do back home, so if you rent a car make sure you get the insurance to go with it.

Vaccinations

None are required.

Water

The local tap water is safe to drink. If you prefer not to, then the bottled mineral water is cheap and widely available.

Sun

This will burn the fair-skinned and those unused to strong rays unless protection is used. A tan from northern Europe is unlikely to be sufficient protection so take things gradually. If snorkelling or diving, the sun's rays penetrate 2 metres (6 feet) below the water's surface. Take plenty of strong sunblock, including the water-resistant kind, and after-sun lotions. Take it gradually at first and wrap up at other times.

Ear infection

An infection can arise from sea water becoming trapped in the ear; small children are especially at risk. Take ear drops with you and talk to your family doctor before leaving if you are concerned about this.

Medical kit

This is a sensible precaution, especially with small children. Take your own supply of medicines if you are a diabetic or on a prescription. Cut-backs may mean some drugs are in short supply, others may be expensive. Take your prescription in case of emergencies.

Mosquitoes

Sometimes mosquitoes and other 'critters' which bite can be quite an irritation; this usually depends on the weather before you arrive. If it has been very wet recently there tends to be an upsurge in the number of mosquitoes. Take an insect repellent just in case you arrive in one of the bad spells. Sprays or roll-on sticks containing DEET are recommended. Malaria has been eradicated.

Poisonous animals

Trinidad and Tobago has a thriving population of snakes a few of which are poisonous, whereas the mongoose, which preys on snakes and which was introduced by the British in colonial days, is almost extinct. Luckily the snakes keep away from areas of human habitation. It is very, very unlikely you will be bitten by a snake, but if you are obtain medical help immediately and remember to describe the snake in as much detail as possible.

Scorpions exist though you are unlikely to see them. Their sting is painful but would not normally prove fatal, except to very small children.

Hospitals

Port of Spain General (tel. 623 2951), on Charlotte Street is the main centre for health care. A new hospital has been constructed at Mount Hope (tel. 662 7153), but is not yet fully operational. On Tobago the Scarborough Hospital (tel. 639 2551), beside Fort George, overlooks the capital, and serves the island.

As mentioned previously the healthcare system has suffered greatly through the government's austerity programme, and is not what it should be. Visitors should not expect the hospitals to be as well resourced as European or North American ones. Remember with most insurance schemes you pay first and reclaim the money later.

A beach near Plymouth on the north-western coast of Tobago, a place where you can frequently find solitude.

THREE

Getting there

By air

There is a fair amount of competition on routes to Trinidad so prices are competitive for flights to Piarco Airport. Tobago has considerably less traffic as the Crown Point Airport has only recently been extended to allow it to take international passengers. This is bound to change in the future given the expansion plans of the country's Tourism Development Authority. On some routes to Tobago you may still have to fly via Trinidad.

From the UK there are direct flights to Trinidad with British West Indies Airlines (BWIA) four times per week via Heathrow Terminal 3. British Airways leaves twice weekly from Gatwick North Terminal. Other possibilities include indirect flights with KLM via Amsterdam, twice a week, or daily flights with American Airlines via Miami. The latter involves an overnight stop in Miami.

London is now linked to Tobago with BWIA, once a week, as are Stockholm and Frankfurt. BWIA's European flights also leave Zurich, Frankfurt, Munich, Cologne and Stockholm for Piarco.

Pan Am fly out of New York and Miami, as do BWIA; the latter make the trip at least twice a day on both routes. BWIA fly to Toronto on Mondays, Thursdays, Fridays, Saturdays and Sundays; Air Canada also fly this route.

BWIA and Leeward Islands Air Transport (LIAT) connect Trinidad and Tobago. BWIA, the national carrier makes the trip five times per day, LIAT once. As the fare is cheap it is also popular, so book as far in advance as you can and always re-confirm.

By sea

Cruise ship passage to Trinidad and Tobago

Both islands now have terminals to cater for cruise ships though traffic is nowhere near as heavy as in other destinations.
Cruise ship operators include the following:

Costa Line Cruises (UK tel. 071 436 9431)
Cunard Line (UK tel. 071 930 4321)
Princess Voyages (UK tel. 071 831 1881).
Royal Caribbean Cruise Line (UK tel. 081 541 5044; USA tel. 305 379 2601).

Yachting

With the low cost of teak and the facility to machine parts on the island, Trinidad is a popular stopping place amongst yachters. See the individual island sections 15 and 16, for details on marinas.

Bareboat chartering

This involves renting a yacht with neither a captain nor crew. The marina at Carenage is the best place to try. As Trinidad is not fully geared up for tourism, you will probably have to negotiate agreements on the spot. Hire costs vary with the size of boat and length of the trip.

Package tours and travel agents

Most tour packages are for Tobago. There are several deals for Trinidad over the Carnival period but little outside of it.

Package holidays offer convenience, cheapness and a fixed price. They take advantage of mass bookings and thereby reduce the price. Christmas and Easter breaks are usually more expensive. Nearly all are based on double occupancy so single travellers may have to pay a surcharge.

Your nearest Trinidad and Tobago Tourist Office will have lists of operators. Here is the list of UK companies who currently organise holidays:

Airwaves, 2A Deodar Road, London SW15 2NN.
Barefoot Traveller, 13 Millpond Court, Bourneside Road, Addlestone, Surrey KT15 2JA.

Caribbean Connection, Concorde House, Forest Street, Chester CH1 1QR.
Happiness Islands, 10 West Park, Harrogate, North Yorkshire.
Hayes and Jarvis, 152 King Street, Hammersmith, London W6 0QU.
Jetlife Holidays, Suite 4, 33 Swanley Centre, Swanley, Kent BR8 7TF.
Kestours, Travel House, Elmers End, Beckenham, Kent BR3 3QY.
Kuoni Travel, Kuoni House, Dorking, Surrey RH5 4AZ.
Lawson International, Hampton Hill, Middlesex TW12 1PS.
Mystique Isles, 19 Royal Avenue House, 1 Royal Avenue, London SW3 4QD.
Speedbird Holidays, Pacific House, Hazelwick Avenue, Three Bridges, Crawley, West Sussex RH10 1NP.
Sunliving, 10 Milton Court, Ravenshead, Nottingham NG15 9BD.
Thomson Holidays, Greater London House, Hampstead Road London NW1 7SD.
Transatlantic Wings, 70 Pembroke Road, London W8 6NX.
Tropical Places, Freshfield House, Lewes Road, Forest Row, East Sussex RH18 5ES.
Worldwide Harlequin Travel Ltd, 124 Handsworth Road, Sheffield S9 4AB.
Continental Villas, 3 Caxton Walk, Pheonix Street, Off Charing Cross Road, London WC2H 8PW.

FOUR

What to take

Clothing

Shorts, T-shirts, and light sportswear are the norm during the day. It is also handy to take a light, long-sleeved shirt to prevent sunburn on your arms in the first few days. Beachwear is frowned upon in town, in restaurants or public buildings. Only the most exclusive of functions will require a jacket and tie. In restaurants, a generally smart appearance is acceptable. Dry cleaning and laundry facilities are cheap and plentiful in town, whilst those on offer by hotels can vary considerably in price. Umbrellas will keep the rain away in the rainy season, whilst a hat is a good precaution against sunstroke.

Money

Over the last few years devaluations of the Trinidad dollar have meant that visitors have been getting better and better value for money. The TT$ is now pegged to the US dollar at $1=TT$ 4.25. As sterling fluctuates against the dollar, one pound varies somewhere between TT$ 6 and TT$ 7.

Most shops and restaurants in the country will take US dollar cash or travellers cheques at the official rate, with any change being given in local currency. Pounds sterling and other currencies usually have to be exchanged at banks. The commission charge at most banks is TT$ 5. Most hotels give the official rate when changing money, but always check first.

Denominations of Trinidadian coins are one, five, ten, 25 and 50 cents, though the latter is quite rare and something of a collector's item. The notes come in TT$1 (red), TT$5 (green), TT$10 (grey), TT$20 (purple) and TT$100 (blue).

Master Card and Visa are widely accepted in the main shopping areas, though some places do not take American Express because of its high commission charges.

It is useful to keep a small supply of quarters if you intend to use the phone.

Electrical adaptors

The islands use 110 or 220 Volts, 60 cycles, so remember to bring suitable adaptors.

Film and photography

If you use a popular brand of print film then you will have no problem finding new rolls, though they are more expensive than back home. If using slides bring as much as you think you will need as the selection is poor in most places. Developing costs are reasonable.

'Foto Magic' High Street, San Fernando has the best range of film. At all shops check the expiry dates of all rolls, as some dealers will have no compunction about selling out-of-date stock.

Food and necessities

Fruits and vegetables can be bought cheaply at any market. Canned and imported goods tend to be a little more expensive. There are numerous bakeries selling a good range of cakes and pastries, which are good value for money, whilst in the larger towns supermarket shopping is available.

Drinks are cheaper than in Europe.

Presents

If you are looking for presents to give out on arrival, the best gift is one from your country of origin. Alternatively, something that is expensive in Trinidad and Tobago such as electrical goods or reading materials would be acceptable, but check the customs regulations first (see next section).

Reading matter

With a hefty amount of VAT added on, books are expensive here. There are several excellant bookshops but, if you can, get your reading material at home. Trinidad has a strong literary tradition and several internationally acclaimed authors, so there is much interesting reading with a strong local theme.

Zenga Longmore's *Tap-Taps to Trinidad* is a good general introduction to the Caribbean. It chronicles the author's leisurely travels around nine islands. In the final chapter she comes to Trinidad. Zenga Longmore's observations are both warm and witty

V S Naipaul's *A House for Mr Biswas* is generally regarded as the author's best novel. It follows the fortunes of a Trinidadian of Indian descent. He begins as a humble sign-writer, becomes a journalist, marries against his wishes and strives to maintain a degree of independance from his wife's overpowering family.

A trio of well maintained fishing boats lying on Toco Bay. Fish make up an important part of the Trini diet.

V S Naipaul's *The Middle Passage* written in 1960 is an account of the author's return to Trinidad, with trips to four other countries. As expected the author's comments are sharp and perceptive.

V S Naipaul's *The Mystic Masseur* is a portrait of a leading local figure who stood for election to Trinidad and Tobago's first parliament. It contains many quips on politicians of the time and their wooing of the electorate.

Eric William's *History of the Peoples of Trinidad and Tobago* gives a good background to the development of the islands. Williams was the country's former Prime Minister, who was also a respected academic and an expert on the history of the Caribbean.

Patrick Leigh Fermor's *The Traveller's Tree* is one of those classics of travel literature and describes the author's travels through 15 Caribbean countries shortly after the war. It is brimming with information on places, wildlife, history, people and their culture.

Shiva Naipaul's *Fireflies* is a moving account of the declining fortunes of a wealthy Hindu family in newly independent Trinidad.

The heroine is 'Baby', the youngest member of the family. She finds herself in a loveless marriage, and as the years progress, witnesses the fall of those around her.

Earl Lovelace's *The Wine of Astonishment* tells of how a small village of Spiritual Baptists reacts to the arrival of the Americans in the war years. Bolo, the community's leader tries to make a stand against the changes he sees going on around him.

Raoul Pantin's *Black Power Day* tells of the events leading up to the 1970 disturbances in Trinidad. Pantin was a journalist at the time.

C L R James's *Beyond a Boundary* is an account of West Indian cricket. A good read for any cricket buff.

Selwyn Ryan's *The Muslimeen Grab for Power* gives the hard facts behind the 1990 coup attempt. It analyses the causes, the events of the six days of violence and the impact it has had on the country since.

Herman Wouk's *Don't Stop the Carnival* is a light-hearted novel set on a mythical island somewhere in the Caribbean, that could well be Trinidad. A Hollywood publicist buys an hotel and leaves the rat-race behind but finds that his troubles are only just beginning.

Amryl Johnson's *Sequins for a Ragged Hem* follows the theme of a homecoming in the Caribbean. Much of the book is set on Trinidad and Tobago and includes a description of Carnival. On the whole though it is not as well written and entertaining as Zenga Longmore's book.

Cote ce Cote la is a phrase-book of all those odd sayings you might chance upon during your visit. It includes such gems as 'cockroach have no right in fowl party', (don't go where you are not welcome); 'Where molasses is fly must be', (birds of a feather flock together); and 'Zandolie find your hole', (know your place).

This is only a small collection. With writers like the Naipauls, Earl Lovelace and others there is a large collection of novels, short stories and poetry to choose from in local literature.

FIVE

Arrival and departure

Immigration

Upon arrival all visitors are expected to complete an immigration card. A carbon copy is returned to you, which you should keep safely until departure when it is examined and collected.

In addition to a passport an onward or return ticket is an entry requirement. Occasionally checks are made to see if visitors have sufficient funds for their stay. Generally there is little delay at immigration.

There is a **departure tax** of TT$50 per person. Children of five years and under are exempt. This is paid after checking in for flights but before entering immigration.

Customs and duty free allowances

Most officials are on the lookout for locals returning from shopping trips in the States and Venezuela; foreigners do not seem to attract the same amount of attention. Visitors are allowed to bring unlimited amounts of foreign currency, 50 cigars or 200 cigarettes or 450 grammes (1lb) of tobacco, one quart of spirits or wine and TT$ 50 in gifts.

The **duty free allowance** for US residents, provided your stay in Trinidad and Tobago has been more than 48 hours, is US$ 400 in merchandise each. This may be pooled by family members. Those over 21 are allowed to include one litre of alcohol. All may carry 100 (non-Cuban) cigars and 200 cigarettes. Those staying for less than 48 hours may carry up to $25 of gifts including 10 (non-Cuban) cigars, 50 cigarettes, 4 fl oz of alcohol (if over 21) and 4 oz of perfume.

For Canadian residents the allowance varies depending on the time spent away and previous duty free claims. After 24 hours of absence

A keenly contested game of basketball in Laventille, a suburb of the capital. All major international sports are played in Trinidad and Tobago – many can be seen on the Savannah over the weekend.

CAN $20 of goods may be carried excluding cigarettes or alcohol; after 48 hours CAN$ 100, including up to 50 cigars, 200 cigarettes, 2 lbs of tobacco and 40 fl oz of liquor; once every calender year after seven days abroad up to $300, of items including the same liquor quotas as for 48 hours. The legal age to import tobacco is 16; 18 for alcohol.

UK and EC residents may bring out 200 cigarettes, 100 cigarillos, 50 cigars or 250 grammes of tobacco. The alcohol allowance is one litre if over 22% proof, or two litres if less than 22% proof of spirits or fortified or sparkling wine. Two litres of table wine may be added, provided the person is 17 or over. Fifty grammes of perfume (two fl. oz) and nine fl. oz of toilet water may be carried duty free.

UK residents are only allowed to bring in another £32-worth of goods, hazily described as gifts in the official literature, though how you can avoid going over this meagre sum is anyone's guess.

Posting gifts home duty free

For the **USA** each present must not exceed US$ 50 in value and should have 'unsolicited gift' written upon the package. It may not include tobacco, liquor or over US$ 5 worth of perfume.

For **Canada** each gift must not be worth more than CAN$ 40 and not consist of alcohol, tobacco or advertising material.

For the **UK** regulations are vague, packages can only contain gifts of 'small value' (judge for yourselves what that means!) and no tobacco or alcohol. Other parcels of up to 22 lbs, marked 'gift' and not more than £5 in value, containing foodstuffs, soap, well-worn clothing and consumable medical supplies will escape duty.

Facilities at airports and harbours

Airports

Piarco International (Trinidad) and Crown Point International (Tobago) airports contain duty-free shops, international telephones, banks, car hire offices, taxi ranks, newsagents, restaurants, bars, airline offices, tourist information desks and, in the case of Piarco, a Bed and Breakfast Association desk.

Buses run on the hour from Piarco Airport, starting at five in the morning, finishing at ten at night. All passengers must buy a ticket before boarding; these can be obtained from the left luggage office. The fare is TT$ 1.50. The taxis cost TT$ 65 during the day; a 50% surcharge is added after midnight or before 0600 hours.

There is a half-hourly bus service out of Crown Point to Scarborough, though most resorts are within a few hundred metres of the airport. The tickets to town cost 75 cents at the left luggage office. Buses run from five in the morning till nine at night. Taxis to Scarborough cost TT$ 40 and to Plymouth TT$ 50.

Harbours

Port of Spain's facilities are located downtown just off Independence Square. There is a shopping mall and bar in the terminal used by cruise ship passengers. The ferry to Tobago docks near the Port Authority which is immediately south of this complex.

Scarborough has recently had its harbour dredged to allow cruise ships to dock there. The ticket office for the Trinidad-bound ferry is on Carrington Street.

Marinas

These only exist on Trinidad, where the facilities are excellent for the Caribbean.

Opposite: *The brilliant colours of those who have chosen to 'play mas' and follow their band. This is no closed shop – if you have a costume, you're in!*
(Photo: Trinidad and Tobago Tourism Development Authority)

Following page, top and bottom: *Part of the Carnival Road March through Port of Spain. An explosion of creative energy and colour. As the people march the bands compete to out-play each other.*
(Photo: Trinidad and Tobago Tourism Development Authority)

Coca-Cola
Coca-Cola
a beer is a
The Devil's
Woodyard

SIX

Where to stay

The Tourism Development Authority prints two accommodation lists: for the winter (high) season and the summer (low) season. In this guidebook the prices are broken down into five categories based on the high season rate for a double room hired on the spot. In most cases this will exclude meals (European Plan). Package holidays tend to be much better value.

To call direct to Trinidad and Tobago, the international dialing code is 809.

Types of accommodation

There is a fair and growing range to choose from. At the top of the range are the resort complexes and hotels built for business travellers. In the middle of the range are the guesthouses and smaller hotels, whilst bed and breakfasts and hostels offer good value for those on a budget. A typical hotel room will have its own bathroom, a double bed, air-conditioning and usually a phone and/or television. Most places offer either self-catering or restaurant/bar.

Resort complexes offer rooms of a high standard and a wide range of activities. These may include sports facilities such as the golf course at the Mount Irvine Bay Hotel or the squash courts and gym at the Grafton Beach Resort, Tobago.

Business hotels concentrate on supplying the needs of the entrepreneur, with conference facilities and good telecommunications. Rooms and service are excellent. These types of hotels are only found on Trinidad. The well-off tourist should not overlook them either – the Hilton, for example, affords beautiful panoramic views of the capital.

A summer school in San Fernando. Over the long summer holidays many Trini children go back to school voluntarily, to study elements of the curriculum that have been causing them difficulties.

Smaller hotels and guesthouses fall into the moderate-to-budget price range and emphasise their friendly, personal service. They are often family-run establishments which are often located away from the beach. Their quality can vary with the efficiency of the manager. Self-catering units are often available.

Camping though not prohibited, is certainly not encouraged or something that a local would do. There are no facilities for this on either island. It is unsafe near any built-up area in Trinidad and could only be recommended in the remotest of places. Tobago is potentially better, but even here it would be unwise to wander far from your tent. There is a YMCA and a YWCA in Port of Spain which provide cheap and basic accommodation, but no youth hostels.

The Bed and Breakfast Association

This deserves a separate mention as it is probably the oldest and most professionally-run association of its kind in the Caribbean. Its membership consists of about 40 host homes on Trinidad and 15 on Tobago. A high standard of accommodation is maintained by regular inspections supervised by members of the Tourist Boards of the two islands.

Each home offers breakfast, with other meals at the discretion of the owner. Often hosts will take visitors on guided tours at little or no extra charge. It does involve living in someone's home but most owners are extremely friendly and helpful. If this type of holiday is one you enjoy then the Trinidad and Tobago Association is highly recommended.

Members display the logo of the Association – a buff coloured coffee cup superimposed onto the silhouette of a house. A booking desk run by volunteers is open during business hours at Piarco Airport.

Renting apartments

As prices are lower in Trinidad than elsewhere in the Caribbean, self-catering is not going to be a great saving unless you are staying for a substantial period. Most places are let on a monthly basis and can be found by looking in the adverts in the local newspapers. Unfurnished apartments are the norm.

A number of villas can be rented out on Tobago; the addresses are given in section 16.

Timeshare and interval ownership

There is none of this kind of accommodation at present but it is possible that this situation will change. The Tourism Development Authority prefers to concentrate on low-rise hotels, however.

Property

Until recently it was very difficult for a foreigner to buy land or property. However, with the advent of recession, restrictions have been eased. It is now possible to buy up to an acre of land when purchasing a residence.

Similarly investment is being encouraged. Up to five acres of land can be bought when setting up a business, or a minority sharehold in a native company can be obtained. The full details are contained in the 1990 Foreign Investment Act. Contact representatives of the Trinidad and Tobago government for more details.

One of many snack trolleys which roam across the Savannah in Port of Spain, selling ice cream and cool drinks.

SEVEN

Getting about in Trinidad and Tobago

Driving

UK, USA, Canadian, French and German driving licenses are all valid up to a period of three months. Driving is by the British system, on the left.

Several of the streets in central Port of Spain are one-way, with roundabouts occurring in many places to ease the traffic flow. Drivers tend to stop where they want to, even if it's just to chat to someone they know, and speeding up to cross as the traffic lights turn red are quirks of road users here. Driving and drinking is widespread.

There is talk, at the time of writing, to make seatbelts compulsory in the front. The highways of Trinidad and roads in southern Tobago are in good condition. The driving conditions in northern Tobago and on the minor roads of Trinidad are noticeably poorer.

The numberplate on a car is an essential guide to a car's function. An 'H' means the car is available for hire; in other words usually a taxi. A 'P' is a privately owned car whilst a 'T' is a truck or large van's registration.

A good street map of Port of Spain is available from most bookshops.

Self drive car hire

The car rental business is dominated by several local companies. There are plenty of outlets on both islands. Rates are better value than in most other countries. Cars can be hired daily, weekly or monthly, at between US$ 35 to US$ 70 per day, and reductions are available for longer periods. Take advantage of the insurance schemes offered. Deposits are usually required; rental includes unlimited mileage but not gasoline.

Hindu prayer flags rise above a house in Plymouth, Tobago; each represents an act of devotion.

Mopeds and bicycles

Some agencies on Tobago are beginning to cater for this market. Bicycles are available in the Store Bay/Crown Point area for TT$ 30 to TT$ 40 per day; try to negotiate reductions for longer periods. Mopeds come at approximately double this rate.

Taxis

Huge numbers of cabs and minibuses ply the roads of Trinidad. These comprise three types of public transport: the private taxi, the route taxi and the maxi-taxi. Only the former is a cab as a European or North American would know them, the rest are dealt with under buses, below.

Cabs can be confused with route taxis which only drive along fixed routes. Private taxis congregate at airports, hotel forecourts and in downtown Port of Spain in Independence or Woodford Squares. If you are in any doubt ask the driver.

Few taxis are metered but all drivers have rate sheets telling them what they can charge between two points. Even if they claim they do not have the list you can rest assured that they know what the correct fares are. Drivers are entitled to levy a 50% surcharge if working between midnight and 6am. Always agree on your fare before you set off.

If a route taxi has no other passengers they will usually agree to deviate from their route but the rate will be comparable to any private taxi. As a rule Trini cabbies are less aggressive and more honest than on other islands.

On Tobago many 'P' registered cars act as pirate cabs; with these taxis the drivers will usually tout for business by waving their arms out the window. Tobago is noticeably harder to get around than Trinidad.

Buses

On Trinidad

They come in all shapes and sizes. The largest are the blue and white buses of the government-owned Public Transport Service Corporation (PTSC). These are very cheap and offer a good selection of services but their lack of frequency means they often lose out to private competition. For these buses you must buy a ticket before you board. These may be obtained at PTSC terminals, some village shops and left luggage counters at the airport.

The PTSC's Express Commuter Service uses new air-conditioned coaches, which travel quickly, stopping at specially selected stops. Fares are slightly increased. It is hoped that some of these buses will be used for special tours and trips outside of working hours. This should make tourist spots increasingly accessible.

The maxi-taxis are privately owned. They are grouped into associations, which can be differentiated by the different coloured stripes along the white minibuses. Slighty more expensive than the PTSC but more frequent, they set off when full.

Route taxis are the most expensive, but by visitors' standards they are still excellent value. These are saloon-type cars which take people along fixed routes, setting off when full. All have 'H' registration numberplates.

Public transport runs from 0500 to 2200 hours on most routes. On the busier roads getting a ride should be possible up to midnight.

On Tobago

Buses are less common, especially in the north of the island. The PTSC operate both the regular and express service, but not regularly enough to make up for the lack of maxi-taxis.

Route taxis (some with a 'P' instead of an 'H' registration), are the most frequent service. The drivers toot their horn and hang their arm out of the window if they see anyone beside the road who looks like they might want a ride.

Inter-island travel

BWIA flies to Tobago five times a day, yet islanders still complain about overbooking. One reason must be the competitive fare, kept low deliberately by the government. A return for an adult costs TT$ 125, children of two to 12 years go for half this. BWIA has offices in Port of Spain and at both airports, but these tickets can be purchased at any travel agent.

For further information call: (Port of Spain) 625 1010, (San Fernando) 652 2379, or (Tobago) 639 3291.

Check-in time is one hour before departure. LIAT also stops in Tobago daily on its way to Grenada.

The Ferry service provides a sailing each way on most days of the year. Two ships are involved in this, the *MF Panorama* and the *MV Tobago*. Typically a boat leaves Trinidad at 1400 and Tobago at 2300; sailing takes six hours. Both ferries carry passengers, cars and cargo. Check-in time is one hour before for those on foot, two hours for vehicles.

Tickets can be obtained from the Port Authority Offices by the quayside in Port of Spain (tel. 625 4906/3055) or Scarborough (tel. 639 2417 passengers, 639 2181 cargo). Opening hours are 0730 till 2100 with a break between 1800 to 1900. Elsewhere they are sold by the Royal Banks in Arima, Chaguanas, San Fernando and Point Fortin. Tickets must be bought two hours or more before the boat sails.

The cost is TT$ 25 one-way or TT$ 80 for a double-occupancy cabin. Children up to the age of 11 go half price; vehicles will be charged from TT$ 25 to TT$ 150 depending on their weight.

As there is an unnecessary amount of hassle involved in buying a ticket, it is strongly recommended that you do so before the day you intend to travel. First you have to queue to obtain the ticket you require then again to pay for it and finally to board. It helps if you have done the first two stages previously.

The boats have a snack area and bar; in addition the *Panorama* has a dining room. They are clean and spacious.

Every few weeks the Port Authority organises an excursion, using one of these boats. Often it's a weekend in Marguarita or perhaps a visit to Grenada's Carnival. These 'specials' are advertised in the local press.

Local ferries operate from Trinidad to Gaspar Grande, which is currently being promoted as 'Fantasy Island'. The ferries cater especially for weekend trippers. Local day cruises also visit this area, see under 'excursions' for details.

Arnos Vale, one of the more exclusive hotels on Tobago.

EIGHT

Streetwise in Trinibago

Crime and safety

Port of Spain has its share of crime. Like other Caribbean nations Trinidad and Tobago has seen the crime rate rise with increased drug smuggling. Avoid the downtown areas and Laventille after dark. Unless you are in a group, take care walking around the Savannah and never walk across it after nightfall. Women should not walk alone after sunset, except in the suburbs of Maraval and St Anns which are generally considered safe. Similar precautions should be taken in San Fernando.

Do not leave belongings lying unattended on beaches or valuables on display in your hotel room, and lock cars. Take sensible precautions. Most people are honest but there is no point in taking risks.

Tobago is a lot more relaxed, there are no large towns, however there are more visitors and it only takes one foreigner with light fingers...

Reporting a theft

If an item is stolen, you must get a police report before you leave if you wish to make a claim. The Trinidad and Tobago police force are polite and helpful to visitors. Listed below are the telephone numbers of the main stations; for others see under emergency numbers in the relevant island section.

Trinidad police

Port of Spain (tel. 625 1261)
San Fernando (tel. 652 2561)
Arima (tel. 664 3563)
Sangre Grande (tel. 668 2444)

Tobago police

Scarborough (tel. 639 2512)
Charlotteville (tel. 660 4388)
Roxborough (tel. 660 4333)

A group of Trinidadian boy scouts. This is one organisation which has thrived since the colonial era ended and attracts members from all ethnic groups.

(Photo: Trinidad and Tobago Tourism Development Authority)

Saving money

Compared to its neighbours, the cost of living in Trinidad and Tobago is very reasonable. Most items are cheaper than at home, but here are a few tips to save on the pennies:

- Bring toiletries, sun block and baby-care items with you.
- Always negotiate your taxi fares before you set off.
- Bring the films you will need with you; develop them when you get back home.
- If travelling around use the buses, they are cheap and go virtually everywhere. Likewise, the ferry between both islands is inexpensive.

Two elderly residents at the beach bar in Speyside, Tobago listening to the West Indies' performance in the Test Match. Any bar in the country will have its quota of well-informed cricket critics.

NINE

Food and drink

Using the bars

Drinks

Seeing and listening to the media here you would get the impression that the two home-made beers were locked in a bitter battle to dominate the market; old favourite 'Carib', versus new boy 'Stag'. Actually they are both owned by the same company. There is no monopolies watchdog here to say otherwise, though so far prices have not suffered. Beers come bottled, with imported lagers, stout and Guinness also available. In the case of the latter do not expect it to taste anywhere as good as genuine Liffey water.

A beer in a local rumshop costs around TT$ 3.50, as you move upmarket the price rises to TT$ 7. Tips are not usually expected or given for drinks alone. Most bars follow the British system, where you go to the bar for service.

Rum is the other popular drink, either with coke, coconut milk or fruit punch. Other spirits and liqueurs are available but are not popular because of their expense.

In the cities and tourist areas it is the norm for women to be out drinking, but in the far corners of both islands an unescorted woman in a rumshop would be a rarity.

Using cafes and restaurants

Until recently the selection of eating out places on Tobago was disappointing, however a number of exciting new places have opened up recently. Port of Spain on the other hand, as a long-established commercial centre has a good choice. There is dining for all budgets. In Port of Spain the price of a restaurant is a good guide to the reputation of its cuisine amongst residents. (See 'Places to eat' for costs and descriptions of cafes and restaurants.)

A snack van in Independence Square, Port of Spain. The roti is the nation's number one snack, a pancake mixture filled with meat and vegetables. Chinese food is also very popular.

Service

This is generally excellent in the more exclusive restaurants. In family-run businesses it tends to be more friendly and informal, but certainly not slovenly. The country does not receive large numbers of tourists and does not take visitors for granted.

Increasingly a service charge of 10% is added. If not, this is the accepted tip if the service was to your satisfaction.

Dress

Bikinis and swim wear are only accepted at the poolside or beach bars. In cafes and fast food outlets, at least T-shirts and shorts should be worn. There are not stringent dress requirements in any of the restaurants, but a smart appearance is expected. This means shirt and trousers for men, but not jackets and ties.

Tipping

This is almost always expected in restaurants but not in most bars; a service charge of 10% is automatically added to the bill when dining. With 15% VAT charges, make allowances in your budget for this. All meal prices quoted in this book include the service charge.

Food

Trinidad and Tobagan cooking

This is hard to define but great to sample. As the country is such a cultural melting pot you can eat around the world here. There are some dishes that are peculiar to this country, and countless others that have been adopted from all over the globe. Locally grown herbs and spices have frequently been added to recipes arriving from overseas. Chinese, European, Creole, Indian and even Arabic dishes are eaten at Trinidadian tables.

A word of warning, however, in most dishes the meat is usually left on the bone, even in the pasties called rotis. Do not feel self conscious about using your fingers. Here are some dishes you can expect to meet:

Roti is the most common snack, it seems as if almost any roadside shop can rustle up one in a few minutes. They consist of a pancake coating wrapped around a filling of meat and/or vegetables, most commonly beef, chicken or potato.

Fried chicken Trinis are chicken crazy. The broiler as it's known locally, is often covered in a spicy batter. It is dished up with coleslaw, rice and salad or, increasingly, chips.

Pepper sauce is offered on the table along with salt and pepper. Be careful as it is as hot as the strongest curry, and can make a meal uneatable unless your mouth is used to it. Soak up the heat by chewing on bread or lots of iced drinks.

A market stall in Rio Claro.

Curried crab usually comes with dumplings. The crab is curried and served whole. The dish will not scorch a hole in your mouth like the pepper sauce, as the curry tends to be mild. It is especially popular on Tobago.

Callaloo leaves come from the dasheen plant. It resembles spinach and sometimes is served as a vegetable with meat or fish. Most eating places offer it as a soup, chopped up or liquidised then flavoured with spices.

Shark and bake is a slab of fish meat, real shark not always guaranteed, served inside a bread roll. A favourite of beach snackbars, especially at Maracas Bay. It can be garnished with hot pepper sauce or Trinidad's curiously sweet-tasting ketchup.

Doubles are another snack food, very cheap and sold at roadside stalls. Originally an Indian dish consisting of chick peas in a mild curried sauce, sandwiched between two pieces of barah, a flavoured bread and fried. **Aloo pie** is similar in consistency, resembling a spiced potato fritter, or there is **sahina**, a spinach patty.

Pepper shrimps are not as deadly as the pepper sauce, the shrimps come in a tangy batter. This dish is served in the universally popular Chinese restaurants.

Pilau can come as a side dish or a meal in itself. The rice is spiced up and mixed with pigeon peas and a range of vegetables or chopped meat.

Coo coo is a gooey mixture of cornflour, okra and coconut milk which accompanies meat and fish dishes.

Breadfruit is another common staple, it is delicious when served up with shredded coconut. Another popular staple is **plantain**. This looks like a large banana, but is fried before being eaten. **Yams** or dasheen, the latter being the root under the callaloo leaf are other carbohydrates.

Tropical **fruit** are cheap and plentiful. Bananas and pineapple are common, along with mangoes. Papayas have an orange flesh and resemble melons on the outside. Sugar apples have a sweet tasting centre with the consistancy of custard.

Other fruit are more common at a juice bar, such as guava or sapodilla. **Mauby** is a soft drink made from the bark of a tree, it has

Opposite: *Bringing in the catch down the Toco Bay jetty. Toco is one of many villages in Trinidad where the majority of the residents make a living through fishing.*

BZ
30

an aniseed-bitter taste. **Sorrel** is made from the petals of this plant. A favoured milk shake is peanut punch.

International cuisine

In addition to the dishes that have been adapted as the islands' own, new restaurants are establishing themselves all the time – Mexican, Italian and Polynesian, for example.

Fast food

Fast food chains are firmly established on Trinidad, Kentucky Fried Chicken and the Pizza chains proving the most popular. Tobago is still free of them. Some islanders want to keep it that way. Others, especially Trinis over for a quick break see them as 'progress'. For more details see 'fast food', section 15.

Angostura Bitters

Famed as the ingredient that makes a gin pink. In Trinidad and Tobago this has not caught on, but a splash is put into drinking water, or as a flavouring to meat. Like coke its formula is a closely guarded secret.

This mixture was first concocted in 1824 during the heady days of the wars for independence in South America. The Bitters were invented by a local doctor in Cuidad Bolivar, a small town on the bank of the Orinoco, then known as Angostura. It was manufactured there until 1875 when production was shifted to Port of Spain.

Angostura Bitters is distilled from a variety of herbs and plants, especially the bark of the Cusparia tree. It was first widely used as a medicine, to lessen the effects of fever or settle stomachs. Nowadays its culinary properties have ensured its continued success.

Buying food

Supermarkets exist in the larger settlements. In the remote areas even the tiniest of hamlets will have a small store. In some places the store doubles up as a rumshop. Locally-made produce is reasonable; imported items are more pricey than in Europe.

Opposite, top: *The Asa Wright Nature Centre lies in abundant rainforest amongst the peaks of the Northern Range. It is one of the best places to come to observe the flora and fauna. Guests may stay on site or just come for the day.*

Opposite, bottom: *Toco Bay village lies in the beautiful and rugged north west corner of Trinidad. Accessible by one road only, it is favoured by those seeking to escape the bustle of the capital.*

TEN

Leisure activities

Tourism on both islands is low key, and there is little in the way of a comprehensive sports holiday. The exceptions to this are the Mount Irvine Bay Hotel and the Grafton Beach Resort, both on Tobago.

Birdwatching and wildlife

This is good on both islands but Trinidad probably has the edge, with the Asa Wright Nature Centre, the Wild Fowl Trust and the Caroni Bird Sanctuary. The latter is the home of the Scarlet Ibis, Trinidad's national bird. Little Tobago and the reef off Buccoo are other notable attractions. To naturalists the turtle nesting sites are unmissable.

Fishing

The potential is good off both islands. For those without their own boat on Trinidad contact In Joy Tours (tel. 622 8974), or the Trinidad and Tobago Gamefishing Association, Maraval Road, Port of Spain (tel. 622 3889).

On Tobago many of the water sports outfits also offer deep sea fishing. For example Paradise Sea Sports of Speyside (tel. 660 5206) or Tobago Marine Sports Ltd of Store Bay (tel. 639 0291). Another contact is Mr Stanley Dillon at Buccoo (tel. 639 8765).

Golf

A comprehensive golfing holiday can be arranged at the Mount Irvine Bay Hotel and Golf Course (tel. 639 8871/3). This is the only course on Tobago. Use is by no means exclusive to members and guests of this resort; non members are also welcome.

On Trinidad there are four courses available. To the north of Port of Spain is St Andrew's Golf Club (tel. 629 2314). Out west lies the Chaguaramas Public Golf Course (tel. 634 4349 ext. 129). In the south of the island are the courses at Brighton Sports Club (tel. 648 7556), at La Brea, and the Trinidad and Tobago Oil Company Club at Point a Pierre (tel. 658 1825).

The grandstand at a Saturday meeting on the Savannah, Port of Spain, where the families of social pre-eminence come to watch the races.

Horse riding

There are two centres on Tobago: Palm Tree Village Beach Resort (tel. 639 4347) and Park Stables (tel. 639 2154). Trinidad has the Bays and Greys Riding Centre (tel. 622 8752).

Scuba

Diving is far superior off Tobago and there are now several operators to choose from. The one most often recommended is Tobago Dive Experience run by Derek Chung at the Blue Waters Inn, Speyside (tel. 660 4341). This operation is probably in the best location, with many dives being close to base. Reef, night and drift dives are on offer. Others are Dive Tobago (tel. 639 3695) and Tobago Marine Sports Ltd (tel. 639 0291).

Through the summer the visibility drops to 50 feet due to the arrival of cloudy water from the Orinoco Delta. From October the clarity improves up to a distance of 120 feet. April to May is the best time, as this coincides with the arrival of large numbers of manta rays in these waters who make interesting diving companions.

Spectator sports

The cricket season runs from January till June, the prime venue being the Queen's Park Oval in the capital. Inpromptu local games are held throughout the nation on weekends.

Race meetings are held regularly on the Savannah, Port of Spain, on Saturdays. A festival atmosphere prevails with numerous stalls providing snacks and amusements between races.

Squash

The Grafton Beach Resort (tel. 639 0191), has newly-built courts on Tobago. In Port of Spain contact the Valley View Hotel (tel. 623 3511).

Snorkelling

Avoid the areas with dangerous currents. The authorities are very good in this respect and mark most potentially difficult areas with signs or red flags.

Buccoo Reef off Tobago is a popular and easily accessible place. It is shallow enough to walk on in places but you would be doing the coral a real favour if you snorkelled as feet have damaged the reef in previous years.

Surfing

January is the best month for waves. Mount Irvine Bay off Tobago and Maracas or Los Cuevas Bays off Trinidad are recommended. For expert guidance contact the Surfing Association of Trinidad and Tobago (tel. 637 0763).

Tennis

The larger sized hotels have tennis court facilities. Most courts are open to non-residents as well as guests though the hire charges for the former may be higher.

Walking

There is plenty of choice in northern Trinidad. Interesting hikes include El Tucuche, the second highest peak at 957 metres (3,072 feet), Maracas Valley and along the Diego Martin Valley. The Forestry Division (tel. 622 4521) and the Trinidad and Tobago Field Naturalist's Club are further useful sources of information.

The Tobago Forest Reserve is another favoured rambling place. On both islands many tour guides offer hikes. You tend to notice much more with a native guide in your party

Windsurfing

Equipment can be hired from operators on both islands. For expert advice call the Windsurfing Association of Trinidad and Tobago (tel. 659 2457).

Availability of facilities

	Trinidad	Tobago
Boating marina	*	
Golf	*	*
Horse riding	*	*
Health clubs	*	*
Jogging track	*	
Sailing	*	*
Scuba		*
Snorkelling	*	*
Spectator sports	*	
Squash	*	*
Surfing	*	*
Tennis	*	*
Wind surfing	*	*

Symbol '' implies facilities available*

ELEVEN

A to Z information

Banks

Opening hours are from 0800 or 0900 to 1400 on Monday through to Thursday. On Fridays the banks are open longer, from 0800 or 0900 to 1200 then 1500 to 1700. In the smaller branches in outlying areas these hours may be restricted.

The banking sector is efficient and foreign exchange is dealt with separately in most places so waiting times are kept to a minimum. The usual commission charge is TT$ 5 but this can vary from place to place.

Many hotels change money at the going daily rate, but check before you make the transaction just in case.

Churches

See under places of worship.

Embassies

British High Commission, Third floor, Furness House, 90 Independence Square, Port of Spain, (tel. 625 2861).

Canadian High Commission, 72-74 South Quay, Port of Spain, (tel. 623 7254).

Danish Consulate General, 72-74 South Quay, PO Box 179, Port of Spain, (tel. 623 4700).

French Embassy, Tatil Building, Maraval Road, (tel. 622 7446).

German Embassy, 7-9 Marli Street, PO Box 828, Newton, Port of Spain, (tel. 628 1630).

Indian High Commission, 87 Cipriani Boulevard, Port of Spain, (tel. 627 7180).

Japanese Embassy, 5 Hayes Street, St Clair, (tel. 622 6105).

Netherlands Embassy, Life of Barbados Building, corner of Edward and Park Streets, Port of Spain, (tel. 625 1210).

New Zealand Consulate, 69 Independence Square, Port of Spain, (tel. 625 3945)

United States Embassy, 19 Queen's Park West, Port of Spain, (tel. 622 6371).
Venezuelan Embassy, 16 Victoria Avenue, Port of Spain, (tel. 627 9823).

Emergency services

These are small islands and you are never far from a police station or medical centre. The fire fighting services are based in the larger population centres. For telephone numbers see in the sections of the island you are visiting.

Hairdressing

A recommended traditional male barbers is in the passage near the union building, a trim here costs TT$ 5. Beauty salons are double or treble this price for women; the larger hotels also offer this service.

Laundry and dry cleaning

Many hotels take laundry or dry clean items for a dollar or two per item, and return them that day if they are deposited in the morning. There are several dry cleaning and Chinese laundry businesses in urban areas and the occasional laundrette.

Philately

At the main post offices there are wall displays of past issues as well as special desks to cater for stamp collectors. The Tourist Office can supply details of current and planned stamp issues. In 1991, for example, five were proposed: ferns, anniversaries, World War Two, religious festivals and the American entry into World War Two.

The Post Office designates other outlets as Crown Agents who also issue stamps. There are two branches of the Philatelic Society on Trinidad, one meets at St Mary's College, Frederick Street, Port of Spain. The other is based down in San Fernando on 78 London Street.

Places of worship

The three main religions in the country are Christianity, Hinduism and Islam. Each of these groups splits into different denominations or sects. Though many beliefs are strongly held there is also a long tradition of tolerance. See under the islands for places of worship in your area.

Tobago is almost exclusively Christian as it traditionally has never had the cosmopolitan population of Trinidad.

Postage rates

International rates are as follows:
TT$ 2 for postcards anywhere.
TT$ 2.25 for letters to Britain, the USA and Canada.
TT$ 2.50 for letters to Europe.
TT$ 2.75 to Hong Kong, Australia, New Zealand and Asia.

Post Restante

Available in Trinidad and Tobago, with the larger Post Offices having a separate desk for this. Mail should be directed to the person 'c/o Post Restante,' then the Post Office, at the relevant destination.

Public holidays

Are plentiful in this fun-loving nation: New Year's Day 1 January; Good Friday and Easter Monday; Whit Monday; Corpus Christi; 19 June is Labour or 'Butler's' Day; Emancipation Day is the first Monday in August; Independance Day, 31 August; Republic Day, 24 September; Christmas and Boxing Day on the 25 and 26 December.

Carnival is celebrated on the Sunday, Monday and Tuesday before Ash Wednesday on which, even if they are not official holidays, little is done – people are too hung over or tired. The Hindu festival of Divali falls in September or October, whilst Eid el-Fitr is in April. Other religious festivals such as Phagwah or Hosay are widely celebrated but are not official holidays.

Shopping

Most goods are slightly cheaper than in Europe, exceptions are books, photographic and electrical goods. Duty free shopping is beginning to take off here, with the 'in bond' system in operation, where the articles are paid for and then delivered to the cruise ship or airport before departure.

Port of Spain's main shopping area is Frederick Street; it is the High Street in San Fernando. The concept of shopping malls has really taken off here. There is one in the centre of Scarborough and many others on Trinidad. Recommended ones are Long Circular, Ellerslie Plaza and West Mall around Port of Spain, or Gulf City near San Fernando.

Shopping hours are from 0800 to 1600 on Monday to Thursday, later on Fridays. On Saturdays most places close at lunchtime, a few stay open into the afternoon.

Souvenirs

Port of Spain is a style-conscious city, locally produced garments can be seen in a large number of boutiques on both islands. The manufacture of batiks is another development as well as hand-painted designs at shops like Niftee's in West Mall.

There are several ranges of prints showing various aspects of life in the country and a thriving artist community whose work can be seen on display in Port of Spain galleries. The larger art shops do mounting and framing.

The craft includes Carnival souvenirs, metal and cocoa pod bangles, ashtrays and bookends. In addition to a large amount of leather work there is some woodcarving.

With there being such a variety of music, tapes and records are a good buy. Ensure the recording is good before you buy. Sanch tapes in particular are noted for their sound quality.

Finally much of the local sugar goes into Trinidad rum, a litre of which is a common souvenir.

Telephone

The international code for Trinidad and Tobago is 809.

Time zones

Trinidad and Tobago is four hours behind GMT and one hour ahead of US Eastern Standard Time.

Tipping

The scourge of the holidaymaker is an unexpected series of surcharges. Ensure you budget for them during your stay. Virtually all restaurants but not bars add a 10% service charge to your bill. Hotels have a 10% service charge and 15% VAT, which effectively means a quarter as much again onto your original costs. You will probably avoid these at smaller more informal establishments but don't count on it.

Thankfully the country has so far been able to absorb the numbers of tourists coming, so widespread tipping is not expected.

TWELVE

Trinidad and Tobago's history

Trinidad's early years

When Columbus and his gold hungry followers sighted Trinidad on 31 July 1498, they began a chain of events that would lead to the utter ruin of the island's peoples. Over the next 200 years the Caribbean would change out of all recognition. The Amerindians would be faced with bleak choices: death by the sword or enslavement.

The island was inhabited from at least 5000 years before Christ. It was named 'Iere' by these people, the land of the humming birds. The inhabitants lived in village communities of a few hundred people. These Amerindians were polytheistic, worshipping or fearing spirits from the sky world, of the earth, and the underworld. They crafted animal and human pottery and a variety of musical instruments.

The tribes practised shifting cultivation, raising maize, beans, cassava, tobacco and cotton. Villages competed for land, often raiding others who were considered a threat, though the wars were never serious enough to disrupt the intricate trade routes that had developed over the preceding centuries. This was a system of barter covering the eastern isles of the Caribbean, the Venezuelan coast, the Orinoco and the Guianas. Food could be traded for hammocks or pearls for tools.

By 1498 there were several different groups on the island: Shebaio, Arawaks, Nepoio, Yao and Carineparoto. Columbus described them as wearing loincloths, feathers and red body paint. In the first encounter a group of Amerindians paddled out in a canoe to examine the Spanish ships. They became alarmed when the Spanish began singing and dancing and shot off a flight of arrows. Columbus's men returned fire and drove the Indians back to shore.

The explorer named the island 'La Trinite', either because of the three peaks he saw, or as an act of thanksgiving after a long and difficult voyage. He was keen to move on as soon as possible and never returned.

Trinidad became a backwater in the Spanish Empire. With no sign of any valuable minerals the early settlers were uninterested in the island. Eventually a governor was appointed, Antonio Sedeno. He gathered a group of adventurers around him and fought a series of battles with the Amerindian tribes. After securing part of the island he saw all his effort ruined when his followers deserted him to seek their fortunes in Peru.

With this Trinidad became a stopping point for raiders looking for slaves to work the pearl beds off the Venezuelan coast. Licenses to hunt for captives were granted if the slavers could convince the Spanish monarchs that the local tribes were savages, or forbidden if the Amerindians had accepted Christianity or were considered 'friendly'. The more tales of cannibalism and barbarism the slavers invented, the more territory they had to prey upon Amerindians. These exaggerated and largely fictional reports have coloured our understanding of Caribbean people to this very day.

Raids and European diseases reduced the population of Trinidad but the tribes continued to resist Spanish colonialisation. In 1592 the Spanish under Domingo de Vera felt secure enough to build the first permanent settlement at St Joseph. By this time, however, Spain's position in the region was being challenged by a new sea power - England.

In 1595 Sir Walter Raleigh led an expedition into the area. He swooped down on St Joseph, destroyed the town and massacred its citizens. He freed the Indian leaders from the settlement's prison, recaulked his ships at the Pitch Lake and sailed on in search of more booty.

The Spanish returned and established plantations and missions. Attempts to convert the islanders to Christianity failed. In 1699 there was a serious rebellion, then in 1708 the missions were closed down by farmers eager to enslave the Indians. Tobacco and cocoa were grown and exported illegally direct to other nations.

In 1757 the administration moved to the coast at Puerto de Espana. There was little real development on the island till 1776 when Governor Manuel Falquez offered grants of land to any Catholic settlers from friendly countries. The new settlers brought large numbers of African slaves for the first time. This scheme was extended in 1783 when 130 acres were offered for each member of the family and 65 acres per slave. Colonists flooded in and a plantation system based on slavery was established.

The lodge and cannon of Fort George, which was built by the British to guard Port of Spain's harbour. It is one of many places that has been restored by the Tourism Development Authority and can be visited free of charge during daylight hours.

Luckily for the subsequent history of the island the period of slavery was comparatively brief. The system did not outlast the memories of the older slaves, so it did not have quite the insidious effects that occurred elsewhere in the Caribbean. Some slaves were brought by owners abandoning other islands, some came on Spanish ships, others were bought illegally off foreign ships by planters eager to enlarge their workforce.

Under Governor Don Jose Maria Chacon the mainly French newcomers were encouraged to take up posts in the islands' Cabildo, a local council. French became the language most commonly used.

The French Revolution brought trouble to the whole region. Refugees, some monarchist, some Republican came to Trinidad. Slaves began to agitate for reform and with the spread of all these conflicting ideas Governor Chacon found it necessary to form a militia. A new period of disorder and violence broke out in the West Indies.

War broke out between republican France and Britain; in 1796 Spain was dragged into the war on France's side. Governor Chacon received some ships and troops to help defend the island against expected attack from the British. This came in Febuary 1797 with 18 ships under Admiral Abercromby. Faced with superior numbers the Spanish burnt their own ships and capitulated. Chacon and his soldiers were sent back to Spain and the people of Trinidad made to swear an oath of loyalty to the British crown.

The next few years were ones of misery for most inhabitants. The first British Governor Picton, was a narrow-minded soldier who saw his job as keeping the island loyal through terror. There were arbitrary arrests and executions. In the Treaty of Amiens in 1802 Spain formerly gave up its claims to Trinidad.

Peace brought about the replacement of Picton. There were thousands of slaves yet the island never saw the wholesale implementation of the plantation system. In 1807 the slave trade was abolished, though unscrupulous estate owners continued to smuggle them in. Although 1834 was emancipation year, freedom did not bring any relief from appalling living conditions.

The scheme whereby freed slaves were tied to the land by an apprentice system fizzled out soon after. Many ex-slaves chose to leave the estates, moving onto uncultivated land or drifting into the towns to get away from the hated plantations. This scarcity of farm workers brought the next phase of Trinidadian history.

The search for labour

In 1848 the British government gave permission for workers to be recruited from India by a system of indenture. The labourers would be tied to the land for a set period, usually five to ten years, after which they would receive a plot of land or a return ticket. The first immigrants actually came from Calcutta in 1845, an event still celebrated as 'arrival day'. Conditions were harsh, the Indians were often cheated and always exploited, even so many settled at the end of their contracts.

The indentured immigrants were regarded with suspicion, and discriminated against by other Trinidadians. They tended to form their own communities in the countryside. Living in groups they have preserved most of their customs. Hindu temples and prayer flags are still a common sight.

Other new arrivals included a mixture of Europeans, Madeirans fleeing from religious persecution, free West Africans and between 1849 and 1866, large numbers of Chinese. The towns grew rapidly in the later 1800s, with the poorer sections of society living in crowded, unsanitary conditions. The railways came and in 1876 the Port of Spain to Arima route began operating. In 1882 it was extended to San Fernando.

By 1889 when Trinidad was united with Tobago, it was already a community of several different peoples. What was lacking was any of the tolerance found today. Festivals like Carnival and Hosay were frequently broken up. The police were recruited in Barbados and hated by the general population because of their aggression. In 1884 they opened fire on the Hosay celebrations killing 12 people. The colonial authorities ruled sternly and racial discrimination was still the order of the day.

The struggle for Tobago

Tobago was probably an island seen by Columbus and named 'Concepcion'. He did not attempt to land. If he had he would have found a mixture of Ciboneys, Caribs and Arawaks. These people's lifestyle was similar to their counterparts on Trinidad, with whom they regularly traded. It is thought they knew the island by the name of Tavaco.

The Spanish ignored 'Concepcion' making no attempt to settle there. It was not until the seventeenth century that serious attempts were made by Europeans to colonise the place. By this time the English, Dutch and French were seeking to expand into this area and the Spanish were no longer powerful enough to stop them.

The English came first in 1625, however, the original inhabitants reacted vigorously to this invasion, wiping them out. In 1628 the Dutch tried to establish a base here but they were massacred by a mixed force of Amerindians and Spanish from Trinidad. The English tried for the second time in 1639 and the Amerindians again drove them into the sea; a group from Barbados met the same fate.

The Duke of Courland was then granted the island by England's Charles I, though by what right is uncertain. Courland was a small Baltic state which is known as Latvia today. The Duke's ambitious project ended in failure. Three times, in 1642, 1650 and 1654 they landed on Tobago and on each occasion, either the Indians or the Dutch destroyed their settlement.

The old mill at Speyside, Tobago. Here the juices were crushed out of the cane at harvest time. The rusting water wheel is one of many reminders of the importance of sugar in Tobago's history.

After this time the Amerindians' ability to expel trespassers from their island seems to have disappeared, their numbers had probably dwindled through exposure to new diseases. As wars flared up in Europe Tobago changed hands continually between the Dutch, English and French. In 1684 these states tried to end the squabbling by making the island neutral in the Treaty of Aix-La-Chapelle, allowing all nationalities to settle there.

This proved to be a disaster as Tobago then became a nest of pirates. The powers in the area felt obliged to intervene and the see-saw battle continued again till Britain got its claim to the island recognised by the Treaty of Paris in 1763.

Britain immediately began to develop Tobago seriously. Thousands of slaves were imported and a plantation system established. The large landowners made huge profits from sugar, rum, cotton and indigo. Their representitives met at a legislative assembly in the capital, Georgetown. Slave uprisings were frequent.

The outbreak of the American War of Independence brought about a brief decline in British fortunes. France, Spain and the Netherlands joined the 13 American colonies ensuring their eventual victory. Britain found her possessions around the world under attack. In 1779 the American navy attempted to take Tobago but the invasion was repulsed when the 36-gun *US Randolph* was blown up with the loss of 315 men.

In 1781 the French attacked and forced a British surrender. The capital was renamed Port Louis and Tobago was theirs till Britain and France found another excuse to go to war. In 1803 the British, victorious in Europe, conquered the island for the last time.

After emancipation Tobago's economy went into decline mainly due to a shortage of labour. The planters' attempts to attract other workers were largely unsuccessful because of the miserly wages they offered. A kind of sharecropping was tried and this worked till the 1870s when a severe recession hit all on the island and landowners reneged on their agreements. With bankruptcy and labour riots afflicting Tobago the British decided to combine it with Trinidad. The local elite objected and managed to retain a degree of autonomy.

The islands unite – 1889 to the present

The last few years of the nineteenth century saw the working classes begin to unionise and the middle classes agitating for a greater say in the running of both islands. Tensions arose as the authorities refused to make any significant changes.

In 1903 the Rate Payers' Association organised a demonstration outside the seat of government, the Red House. A riot began when the crowd's representatives were refused entry. The Red House was burnt down and armed police dispersed the crowd, killing 18. Finally in 1913 a Borough Council was established giving a limited amount of political expression.

The country's industrial base was built up at this time. Oil was discovered at Guayaguayare in southern Trinidad and with the invention of automobiles and oil-fired ships there was a steadily growing demand for it. Britain wanted a dependable supply from within its own Empire.

In World War I West Indian soldiers abroad experienced much discrimination, whilst at home shortages led to hardships for the poor. When the war ended a series of strikes hit the colony. The government introduced a series of harsh laws and were not above calling in troops to restore order.

Between the wars two important reformers emerged. The first was Captain Arthur Cipriani; he was from a well-off family and had served in Africa during World War I. Upon his return he began to campaign for the rights of the poor and disenfranchised. He was elected to the Legislative Council and never lost his seat. He tirelessly fought for what he believed in till his death in 1945.

In the severe depression of the 1930s another man arose who led the unions' struggle to improve conditions for the working class, which even the official reports recognised as appalling. This was Uriah 'Buzz' Butler, a Baptist Preacher. He organised several strikes and went to prison for it.

World War II brought Americans to Trinidad. In return for a fleet of destroyers to escort convoys over the Atlantic, the USA leased a number of bases around the Caribbean. In Trinidad they established a large camp at Chaguaramas and an air base at Waller Field. The Americans changed many attitudes on the island. They offered higher wages and had none of the stuffiness of the British colonial authorities. The rumshops, brothels and strip joints did good business in between the raids by the police. Perhaps most importantly the Americans cast aside the oil drums which local musicians were soon to put to such good use.

The first election under universal suffrage was held in 1946. Many of those elected were little more than rogues who promised all and delivered little, though men like 'Buzz' Butler were subsequently elected.

It was only in the elections of 1956 that a strong political party emerged. This was the People's National Movement (PNM) led by Dr Eric Williams. Williams was an academic who had returned from a successful career abroad. He addressed crowds at the so-called 'University of Woodford Square' before the elections, and was to loom large in Trinidadian politics till his death in 1981.

Williams's PNM formed the government of the colony and steered it towards independence which came in 1962. For the next few years the PNM were kept occupied by the stagnating economy.

The first challenge to democracy came with the rise of the Black Power marches in 1970. Many were rightly angered by continued discrimination against blacks in the workplace. As the PNM had done little to end this they were seen as collaborators with big business. With increasing disorder a state of emergency was declared. A group of soldiers, led by Lieutenants Shah and Lassalle mutinied in support of the demonstrators and armed themselves, setting out for the city. The government could well have been toppled if the Coast Guard had not remained loyal and turned their guns on the rebels.

This innocuous looking building was the base of the Muslimeen, who drove out of here, armed to the teeth, on 27 July 1990. In their ill-fated attempt to overthrow the elected government several people were killed and the Prime Minister was briefly seized and held hostage.

During the 1970s Tobago complained loudly about the neglected state of their facilities. Led by veteran politician A.N.R. Robinson they finally obtained their own House of Assembly with wider powers than they had had before.

The 1970s saw the great oil boom hit the nation. There was suddenly money everywhere. The standard of living rose and lavish new projects were unveiled, however, this was matched by corruption and a crass materialism. After 1981 the economy began to slide into recession. The PNM at this time were without Williams; they failed to halt the country's worsening problems.

In the 1986 election the unthinkable happened, the PNM lost. Under A.N.R. Robinson, a new coalition of older groups, the National Alliance for Reconstruction (NAR) was formed. It was a landslide victory of 33 seats to 3. In power the NAR were forced to bring in tough austerity measures. These gained the support of the business community but alienated thousands of Trinidad's poorer families. The NAR survived a coup attempt but was fatally weakened by a party split over its economic policies.

Back came the PNM in the 1991 election. Under Patrick Manning they took 21 seats. The United National Congress, formerly part of the government, gained 13 seats, leaving the NAR rump with only two seats. Manning has announced that one of his priorities is a crackdown on crime and drug smuggling.

Coup d'etat!

On the evening of Friday 27 July 1990 as most citizens of Port of Spain were on their way home from work, gunfire and explosions rocked the capital. In a series of dramatic moves, a small group of radical Moslems – the Muslimeen – took over key buildings in the capital. The police station was bombed, the TV station seized and the parliament stormed. Several died in the assault.

The country awoke to find most of their government held hostage and the police and army struggling to maintain law and order as looting broke out. A stand-off situation developed; after six tense days the Muslimeen surrendered expecting an amnesty.

The whole affair came as a profound shock to the nation. How could such a group smuggle in a large cache of arms undetected? Why did the uprising take the authorities so completely by suprise? What would have happened to the nation if the Muslimeen had succeeded?

There has been much discussion on how to move forward. Many feel that politicians should do more than condemn the rebels. The democratic process must be promoted rather than taken for granted. The ballot box is of small comfort to the poor if basic welfare and health provisions are neglected.

Perhaps the greatest tribute to the national character is that there was no backlash against the Moslem community. All Trinidadians and Tobagonians have pulled together to try to put the events of July 1990 behind them.

THIRTEEN

The islands today

The political scene

Trinidad and Tobago has enthusiastically elected representitives to a democratic parliament since 1946. Apart from serious hiccups in 1970 and 1990 it has maintained a representative government throughout. Dr Eric Williams was the nation's leader for 25 years from 1956 and was an immense influence on its early years.

The traditional party of power is the People's National Movement (PNM), who have only lost one election, in 1986. The National Alliance for Reconstruction (NAR) was an amalgam of several political groups who came together as a united front to challenge the PNM. Splits developed over the party's economic policies and the style of its leader, Robinson. The United National Congress left the NAR to fight the 1991 election separately.

This split in the government helped the PNM to win convincingly. The PNM's views are to the left of the NAR. Previously voting was on racial lines, with the PNM being seen as the party of those of African descent. Politicians sought to exploit the prejudices of the voters though this was broken down in 1986. Most people hope that elections will continue to be fought over issues of policy and not race.

The lower House of Representatives has 36 seats, 33 of which are held by the government. The upper Senate has 31. The President's role is largely ceremonial. Trinidad and Tobago is a republic yet still an active member of the Commonwealth.

Tobago has had its own House of Assembly which has some control over the island's finances. The former Prime Minister, A.N.R. Robinson comes from this island. Every now and then there are grumblings on Tobago of secession, of going it alone with the revenues gained from tourism. At present a majority of Tobagonians seem content with the union.

One subject of heated debate was whether the country needed its army. After the troubles of 1970 it was seen by some as a potential threat to democracy. Yet in the coup of 1990 the army redeemed itself, and without it the government would probably have collapsed.

Local politics involve a lot of mudslinging, trying to label opponents corrupt or inefficient. The previous NAR government accused the PNM of financial mis-management during the boom years. The PNM were even accused of being involved in the 1990 coup attempt though no evidence was presented to prove this. It is a sad fact that the politicians who make these comments do not realise the damage they are doing to the institution they sit in, let alone their own careers.

The physical environment

Both Trinidad and Tobago were part of the Venezuelan mainland several thousand years ago. They have highly fertile soil. Before European colonialisation the ground was covered with rainforest and swamps. Cultivation has cut back the wooded areas but by no means destroyed them. Trinidad is closest to Venezuela, which is seven miles away at the narrowest point, separated by the waters of the Dragon's Mouth and the Serpent's Mouth. The shores of both islands are influenced by the waters of the Orinoco.

Trinidad is 80 kilometres (50 miles) long from west to east at its furthest point, or 58 kilometres (37 miles) from the north to the south coast. It has two main ranges of mountains the Northern and Southern Ranges. The former are more dramatic and imposing with the two highest peaks on the island, Cerro del Aripo 961 metres (3,083 feet) and El Tucuche 957 metres (3,072 feet); the latter is a popular hikers' destination. There are large areas of marshy land of which the most famous are the Caroni and Nariva swamps. Salybia Reef is the only coral formation of significance on Trinidad; it lies off Toco on the northern coast.

To the west of Port of Spain, Trinidad has its own satellite islands. The largest are Gaspar Grande, Monos, Huevos and Chacachacare. Gaspar Grande has a system of caves.

Tobago lies 34 kilometres (21 miles) north east of Trinidad and is 42 kilometres (26 miles) long, 16 kilometres (9 miles) wide. The northern end is more hilly with Main Ridge reaching a height of 600 metres (1,890 feet). The southern portion is flatter with a series of low hills leading down to wide sandy bays.

Buccoo Reef is Tobago's most accessible, with daily excursions running from Store Bay. It has suffered damage over the years. Divers

A group of children out admiring the view from San Fernando Hill. Previously quarrying scarred much of this notable landmark, which is now preserved as a park.

may find the reefs around Speyside, Man-of-War Bay and Charlotteville more spectacular. Visitors are urged to take care to leave the reef as they found it.

The economy

In 1857 the world's first oil well was drilled at La Brea. During 1914 the colony's first refinery opened at Point-a-Pierre and since then oil has been a major part of the country's economy. It was oil that brought about the boom in the 1970s and an over-reliance on the same that brought such a heavy crash in the 1980s. Today there is a second refinery at Point Fortin and a total output of 150,000 barrels per day.

Trinidad has one of the largest industrial bases in the Caribbean. Steel, ammonia, urea, and methanol are all produced and exported. Virtually all the industries are situated in the south of the country.

Asphalt continues to be exported from the Pitch Lake at La Brea. There are continuing attempts to move away from the over-reliance on oil, but apart from bitumen and natural gas there has been little development of mineral deposits.

With the introduction of the Foreign Investment Act the government hopes to attract more overseas money. Foreigners can now establish their own ventures. The bureaucracy involved has been greatly reduced. Overseas investment for 1990 was approximately US$ 100 million.

Agriculture makes up about 5% of the gross domestic product. Sugar, cocoa and coffee have declined over the past few decades, as has the cultivation of citrus fruits and coconuts. Part of the problem is that labour costs are higher than on other islands.

Trinidad and Tobago is continuing to develop its tourism, but not in an irresponsible way. Both islands are being developed but more emphasis is being put on Tobago, where the plan is to nearly double the number of hotel rooms by 1994. Along with this expansion would have to come an improvement in the infrastructure of both islands and better air links with Tobago. About 200,000 visitors come each year.

Inflation hovers at around 5%; unemployment is beginning to drift down from 20%. There is no social security for the jobless. The growth rate in 1990 was 0.7%. After some hard knocks the country seems to be emerging from a long recession.

Flora and fauna

Between Trinidad and Tobago there are 420 species of birds, including 15 different species of hummingbird. Not all of these are endemic to both islands. Sixty different types of bat and 620 species of butterfly have also been recorded, so it is not surprising that naturalists have been coming here for years. It is hard to find so much variety in such a small area as this.

Nor is there any scarcity of larger species: brocket deer, peccaries or quenk, armadillo, red howler monkeys, agouti and ocelots. Poisonous snakes live in the remote areas but these are difficult to find, whilst caymans live in the swamps.

There is a greater awareness about the environment than might be found on other Caribbean islands, though you may find it hard to believe when you see the piles of litter by the roadside. Around half the land is still forested and much has been protected. There are six national parks on Trinidad and two on Tobago - Buccoo Reef and the rainforests; the latter is the oldest reserve in the western hemisphere.

In addition there are many recreation parks, conservation areas and scientific reserves, as well as a series of natural landmarks. Certain places have gained an international reputation, such as the Asa Wright Centre, the Caroni Swamp and Little Tobago.

Within the rainforest is an enormous amount of plant life. Huge thickets of bamboo grow beside all manner of fruit-bearing trees: cocoa, papaya, mango, banana, cashew, almond and breadfruit. From December to March the majestic immortelle trees burst out in orange flowers; April sees the brilliant yellow blooms of the poui tree. The scarlet Chaconia, the national tree, is another common sight amongst the ferns, frangipangi, orchids, heliconias and poinsettias.

Five of the world's seven species of sea turtle nest on the country's beaches. Some choose the north coast of Trinidad but others the bays of Tobago. Expeditions to watch the nesting after dark are frequently arranged.

The Hosay festival is held in St. James, one of Port of Spain's suburbs. Tassa drummers lead a procession, escorting representations of minoretted tombs called tadjahs.

FOURTEEN

The people of Trinidad & Tobago

A varied background

As outlined in the chapter on history the islands have been shaped by a large number of influences. Of the 1.3 million people, the two largest racial groups originate from Africa or India. Three European groups, the British, French and Spanish throughout the colonial years influenced the culture enormously.

Pure blooded Amerindians disappeared last century as a distinct group. However, some people, especially in the Arima area of Trinidad still claim a partial descent from them. Historically the Afro-Trinidadian is more urbanised whilst the Indians settled in the south of the country where land was available after a period of indentured labour. There is friction between the two communities which can flare up during elections when politicians try to divide the people to win votes.

Whites now comprise only a tiny percentage of the population and tend to mix less with other groups. Some still have large landholdings, others run businesses; very few could be considered poor.

It was the Africans who developed the French Carnival into what it is today. They have been the driving force behind calypso, soca and steel band music. The Indians retain many of the practices of their homeland. Their religions and festivals are recognised whilst their cuisine has gained enormous popularity throughout the country.

The Chinese are another group which have had enormous influence on the nation's cooking. There is now also an identifiable Lebanese community in Port of Spain. Generally racial distinctions are blurring on Trinidad and discussing race and background is not the minefield it can be elsewhere.

Tobago developed separately till 1889. It does not have the ethnic diversity of its sister island. The 50,000 people here are predominantly of African descent.

Catholic Church, Port of Spain. For centuries the Roman Catholic religion was the dominant faith in Trinidad. Nowadays this is no longer the case – the Hindu and Moslem religions, in addition to evangelical churches, all have a large amount of influence amongst the population.

There are more things that bind Trinis together than hold them apart. They share a common optimism towards life, the desire to keep smiling and have a good time no matter how bad things are. 'Fetes', the local word for a party, are organised at the drop of a hat. No groups shun Carnival, everyone joins in and has a good time. Growing up in such a society most Trinis become confirmed hedonists, full of bravado and brimming with confidence.

Values and beliefs

A believer with a microphone exhorting people to listen to their message is no strange sight in Port of Spain. On many occasions, the bandstand in Woodford Square is occupied by the faithful looking for converts. People pass by amused or listen with interest.

This is a country of three main religions: Christianity, Hinduism and Islam. Christianity predominates in the other Caribbean islands. All vie and compete with each other, yet co-exist with amazing tolerance. People gather to celebrate each other's religious festivals with gusto and the state takes a tolerant view of all the faiths. Sectarianism takes the form of letters where correspondents politely disagree with each other. The 1990 coup was seen as a political and not as a religious issue.

All view the increase of drug use and violent crime with dismay, yet disagree on the solution. Some suggest greater police powers, others more social welfare; the more traditional blame the permissive society and greed. Reminiscing about the good old days happens here just as much as anywhere else.

Folklore

Amerindian legends say that the Chiman tribe used to live on the site of the Pitch Lake. They chose this place because the land was bountiful and they lived well but became vain. The Chimans began hunting the humming birds which were protected by the gods and as punishment they were buried beneath a lake of asphalt.

Another legend claims that Mount Naparima is the body of Haburi, an Indian hero. African legends talk about Duennes or the spirits of unbaptised children who cause mischief in the forest, Madam Diablesse a she-devil who lures men to their death or Lagahoos – werewolves.

Tobagonians mention Mamoo Brebna, an African slave whose power was so great he was able to stop the sugar mills from functioning. If his master tried to punish him then the master's wife would feel the pain of the blows.

'Bush' medicine

Some traditional cures are still used from time to time, here are a few of them:

Aloes, for colds and headaches.
Bardaloo, mixed with lime juice and pot soda it is used as a cure for worms.
Fever grass, for fevers and colds.
Soldier's tea, kills the appetite.

Handicrafts

The main crafts are leather work and metal beating, Independence Square in Port of Spain is a good place to view such articles.

Carnival

Unleash a year's artistic and creative energy onto the streets of towns and villages across the nation and you have the two day Carnival. An explosion of colour, combining the finest in music, dance and design Trinidad and Tobago have to offer.

Carnival is a time when all sections of society come together, regardless of age, race or religion. It captures the national spirit more than any other event. Originally a French festival covering the two days before Ash Wednesday, it has been enthusiastically adopted by all.

Port of Spain is the centre of the event. There are dozens of clubs who adopt a theme for the coming year and then, after extensive research design the costumes for the hundreds of followers of that band. Peter Minshall has gained an international reputation for his work. Foreigners are welcome to masquerade or 'play mas'. Each band is led by a King and Queen whose costumes are the finest of them all. These monarchs parade in front of the crowd from the Friday prior to the opening. On Dimanche Gras (Sunday), the King and Queen are chosen to lead the forthcoming festivities.

The Jour Ouvert, or official start is at 0400 on the Monday morning, but since the Christmas before there will have been a series of calypso and steel band concerts under canvas which will have been heightening expectations and building up the atmosphere. Joovay is not when the best costumes appear, rather, home-made ones of a comical nature. The crowd march and dance till shortly after daybreak.

The Queen of a band displays her beautiful and intricate costume as she moves across the stage in the Carnival Monarch competition. Supporters cheer from the highly prized seats in the grandstand around her.
(Photo: Trinidad and Tobago Tourism Development Authority)

Later that day the road marches begin along specially cleared routes. People march behind the calypso bands who do battle with each other to see who has the most popular tune. The marches continue on the Tuesday in even greater numbers. On this day there are the final band competitions. By Ash Wednesday people are exhausted but some are already reflecting on how to make sure they have the winning ideas for next year.

If you are interested contact one of the following groups:

The National Carnival Commission, 92 Frederick Street, Port of Spain, (tel. 809/623 7600) for general information.

The National Carnival Bands Association, 15 Kitchener Street, Woodbrook, Port of Spain, (tel. 809/ 623 8870) for information on costumes and playing mas.

Trinbago Calypsonians Organisation, Cruiseship Complex, Wrightson Road, Port of Spain, (tel. 809/ 627 8021) for information on calypso tents.

Future Carnival dates

22-23 February 1993
14-15 February 1994
27-28 February 1995
19-20 February 1996
10-11 February 1997.

Festivals

These are in plentiful supply in the Trini calendar. All festivals are keenly followed by a large section of the people and some feel that they have a stronger cultural than religious significance.

Hosay derives from the Shiite Moslem, Hussein festival. It commemorates the murder of two of the Prophet's grandsons during the Holy Wars when the word of Islam was spread throughout the Middle East. Elsewhere the event may be accompanied by mourning but here Hindu practices such as tassa drumming are an integral part of the marches which last for four nights.

The focus of everything is undoubtedly the appearance of the Tadjahs on the last day. These are huge mosque structures representing the tombs of Hussein and Hassan. They can reach up to 15 feet in height and are covered in bright paper, tinsel and glass. Marchers follow behind the drummers and the Tadjahs.

At the end of the day the Tadjahs are broken up and cast into water to represent the funeral ceremony. The largest Hosay march is in St James, one of the suburbs of Port of Spain; others occur in San Juan, Tunapuna, Arima, Couva and San Fernando. Tobagonians do not celebrate this event.

Deepa Divali – in October or November Hindus celebrate to honour Lakshmi the goddess of light. On this day countless deyas, small pots containing a wick and coconut oil are hung outside houses, on fences or around the temple. The lights must be maintained all night. Singing and dancing competitions are held in the preceding days, gifts are exchanged, prayers for peace uttered and a special sacrificial meal, the prasad, prepared.

Phagwa is the Hindu festival to celebrate the victory of good over evil. In the run up to the day Chowtal singing competitions are held and bonfires lit to signify the destruction of evil. On the day there are marches and dancing during which Abeer, a purple vegetable dye is sprayed over revellers.

Five Moslem girls in Woodford Square, Port of Spain. Part of a recruiting drive, giving out leaflets on the Islamic religion, they pause to pose for the camera. Seeing the amount of mutual toleration between the different faiths of Trinidad is a refreshing experience.

Eid-ul-Fitr is the feast that comes at the end of Ramadan, it falls between April and June. This festival is more subdued than others, it is celebrated in the mosque or in the home.

Independence, Emancipation and Republic days are all national holidays marked with concerts, sporting events or marches. The people of Arima celebrate the Santa Rosa festival, a mixture of Christian and Amerindian beliefs. Santa Rosa became the first saint of the new world and is honoured in a procession every August when her 230-year-old statue is paraded through the streets.

Other events are bizarre by comparison. Over Easter Tobago holds its goat and crab races, which never quite work out as planned. In March the Bath Tub Derby is held in western Trinidad on the Mayaro-Nariva River. The brightly costumed crew have to paddle their unorthodox boats across the finishing line.

Music

The music of Trinidad and Tobago is exported around the world. Calypso is a blend of African and European influences with the former dominating. The origin of the word is disputed. The early calypso bands had a bad reputation as they were the rallying point for street gangs and the songs often accompanied stick dancing, or more accurately, stick fighting.

Calypso was also used to ridicule authority and public figures by its irreverent lyrics. Gradually through sponsorship, the bands became more respectable, though the outspokenness of the lyrics has not. Nowadays it dominates the air waves on the run up to carnival. Some artists such as David Rudder are known around the world and Lord Kitchener and Sparrow have been famous for years.

The steel drum, or pan as it is known locally, also had a long fight before it was accepted by mainstream society. It emerged at the end of World War II. With Carnival forbidden someone realised discarded oil drums could be tuned to take a huge range of notes. The pans themselves are accompanied by a rhythm section.

Steel bands are starting to open their pan yards to spectators. Leading the way are the Amoco Renegades who play every Friday night in downtown Port of Spain. Festivals are organised to show off the versatility of the steel band, namely the Pan-classical and the Pan-jazz concerts.

Soca is a blend of calypso and soul. It is more commercial and competes in the pop industry with other types of dance music. 'Taxi' are one of the favourite bands of this type at present.

Tassa drumming is exerting a greater and greater influence on the local music scene. This originated in India and is often seen at street parades. Parang is a type of folk music which is particularly popular at Christmas. Traditional Indian music is still battling to be accepted by the population at large, but can be seen in a number of local halls around Trinidad.

In Trinidad and Tobago you do not dance to all these different types of music, you wine. A wine is a rhythmic, gyrating movement, very different to the jerky routines usually seen in European discos. If you have never been on this kind of 'wine' before, there is still time to loosen up those bones before you get out there.

FIFTEEN

Trinidad

Introduction

Separated by only a few kilometres of water from the South American continent, Trinidad is utterly dwarfed by this great landmass. Yet by Caribbean standards it is the largest island in the Lesser Antilles.

Port of Spain is by far the largest settlement, containing over 350,000 people if you include all the suburbs. It has continued to prosper since the capital was moved from St Joseph to the coast in 1757. Today it is a bustling and vibrant city.

The landscape varies widely around the island. The beaches of the north coast attract many Trinis looking for a weekend of relaxation. To reach these from Port of Spain you have to drive through the rainforest-coated Northern Range. The land south of the capital turns marshy, becoming the Caroni Swamp, a wildlife haven.

Further south lies the area where the nation's industrial base is concentrated, around the Point Lisas industrial estate, and the Pointe-a-Pierre oil refinery. Before reaching San Fernando, the state's second city, the oddly-shaped San Fernando Hill is a notable landmark. Continuing down to the south west point you pass the Pitch Lake, one of the oddest natural wonders. Point Fortin is another industrial area.

Central Trinidad is primarily agricultural; sugar, cocoa, coffee and citrus fruits grow in abundance. Here, outside New Grant lies another strange natural phenomenon, a dozen miniscule volcanoes bubbling and oozing mud. The west coast has long stretches of beach and is another favoured recreational area.

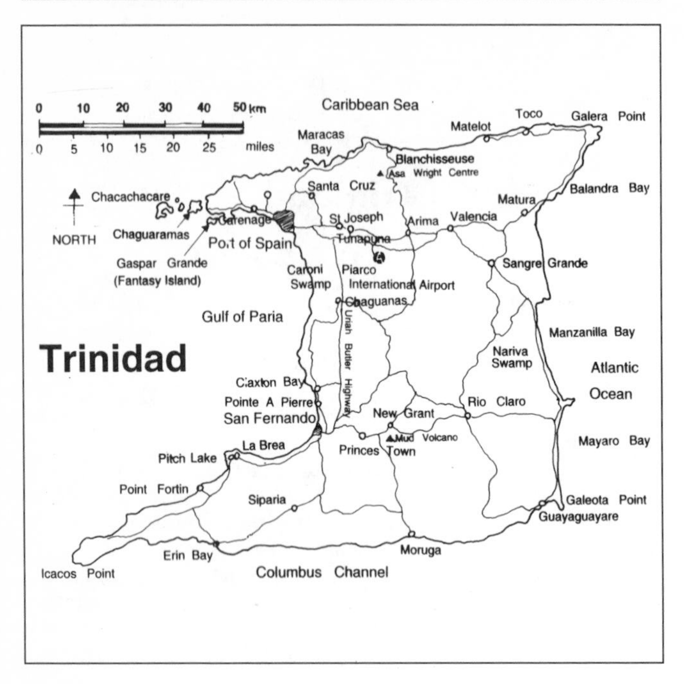

Arrival

By air

Here is a brief summary of flights into Piarco International Airport:

Europe: BWIA fly direct from London four times a week; British Airways makes the trip twice. KLM fly from Amsterdam, whilst BWIA link to Frankfurt, Munich, Zurich, Cologne and Stockholm. American fly via Miami.

North America: Piarco International Airport is linked to Miami and New York. Air Canada has direct flights to Toronto. BWIA flies to the above cities daily.

South America: Trinidad is linked to Margarita and Caracas in Venezuela. The Caracas to Piarco route is operated by PanAm and Viasa, local operators fly to Margarita.

Trinidad's literary son - VS Naipaul

Vidiadhar Surajprasad Naipaul grew up in a Hindu household in central Trinidad. He was educated at Queen's Royal College in Port of Spain then left the country for Oxford University. After deciding to settle in Britain he began writing. His first four books were about Trinidad: *The Mystic Masseur, The Suffrage of Elvira, Miguel Street* and *A House for Mr Biswas*. Many Trinidadians have been offended by the harsh things he has said about the country.

In 1960 he returned to Trinidad and wrote *The Middle Passage,* the first of a series of travel books. Again the acerbic comments flowed, Naipaul and Trinidad have seemed to agree on a mutual separation. He has continued to write a series of much-acclaimed travel books with a heavy political slant. Naipaul is now a writer of international renown; he received a knighthood in 1990.

Naipaul has a great ability to get down to the heart of the matter, and his work is full of insights on Trinidad, yet it is tinged with an edge of gloom and despair. Whatever his thoughts of his native land, his success has been an inspiration to many local writers.

At the airport

The terminal has all the services expected of a major international airport: newspaper and bookshops, duty free, bank, post office, tourist information desk (from which hotel reservations can be made), a bed and breakfast information desk (which will arrange accommodation with its members), and car hire outlets. Upstairs there is a snack bar selling a range of meals and drinks; the licensed bar is next door.

By sea

Port of Spain does not get the volume of cruise traffic of other Caribbean nations, but this is probably a boon as the associated tourist sharks are not present. The cruise ship port takes you right into the heart of the capital, on Wrightson Road just off Independence Square. There is a modern shopping mall in the warehouse building at the point of disembarkation. In addition to a wide range of stores and boutiques selling souvenirs, there is a restaurant and bar.

Yachting Marinas

Trinidad and Tobago has gained a good reputation amongst the yachting fraternity for the ease with which repairs can be made and spare parts obtained. With a manufacturing base on the island many parts can be machined here. Furthermore, prices tend to be a lot more

The view over Laventille, looking down from Fort Picton. Down below, youths from the nearby houses gather for a game of football.

reasonable than at other places in the English-speaking Caribbean. The price of teak is low as Trinidad has its own supply in the rainforest. Insurance is also reduced because the island is outside the hurricane belt.

The following places cater for incoming boats:

Port Authority, Wrightson Road, Port of Spain, (tel. 809 623 2901), provide unlimited water, garbage diposal, bathrooms and a security patrol for US$ 12 per day, after the fourth day this rate drops to US$ 7.
The Yachting Association, Chaguaramas, (tel. 809 634 4376), offer berths for 20 boats, water, bathrooms and electricity for US$ 12 per day.
The Trinidad Yacht Club, Bayshore, (tel. 809 637 4260), have facilities for 50 yachts including water, electricity, security guards and a restaurant. The cost is US$ 15 per day, plus 15% VAT and a temporary membership fee.
Trinity Yacht Facilities, Chaguaramas Bay, PO Box 3163 Carenage, (tel. 809 634 4303), have the equipment for outhaul and storage. On

site are a 50-ton marine hoist and a skilled workforce. Water and electricity are free.

Transport

Taxis

The taxi fare from Piarco to Port of Spain is TT$ 65 and it is TT$ 120 to San Fernando. Taxi drivers have lists of fares for different destinations and this seems to be the preferred way of deciding the fare rather than by a meter. After midnight and before 0600, drivers are entitled to add half as much again to the overall cost.

Try not to confuse private taxis with the shared route taxis.

Car hire

There are several agencies, all locally owned. The two with a branch at the airport are dealt with first.

Auto Rentals Ltd have offices at the airport (tel. 669 2277), the cruise ship complex (tel. 624 8687), and at Uptown Mall, Edward Street, Port of Spain, (tel. 623 7368). Rates start at TT$ 150 daily, TT$ 900 weekly, rising to TT$ 190 daily, TT$ 1,140 weekly.

Singh's Auto Rentals' offices are located at the airport (tel. 664 5417) and at 7-9 Wrightson Road, Port of Spain (tel. 625 4247). Their rates vary from TT$ 160 to TT$ 260 daily or TT$ 960 to TT$ 1,560 weekly.

Dunmore Enterprises Ltd is based in San Fernando (tel. 657 5296). Small automatic cars are available at TT$ 185 per day or TT$ 1,500 per week.

Furness Rentals Limited (tel. 627 0658) is located on Independence Square. The daily rate is TT$ 195 to TT$ 285, the weekly is TT$ 1,200 to TT$ 1,800.

Premier Auto Rental Ltd (tel. 624 7265) currently offer the most competitive rates at TT$ 120 per day or TT$ 630 per week for a small car with a manual gearbox.

Other companies that can be called are **Lazzari Rentals Ltd** (tel. 652 3458), **Quality Motors Ltd** (tel. 652 2795), **Southern Sales and Service Co Ltd** (tel 627 7328), **Bacchus Taxi Service** (tel. 622 5588), **Toyota Rent-a-Car** (tel. 628 5516), **Tragarete Car Rentals** (tel. 622 3025), **Carr Rental Ltd** (tel. 624 1028) and **Econo Car Rentals** (tel. 622 8072). There are many more; the Tourism

Development Authority produce a handout which lists all the rental agencies.

It is strongly recommended that all motorists take the insurance schemes on offer. Expect to have to pay a deposit.

Motorbike and bicycle rental

This has not caught on here. Some of the car rental agencies may have mopeds available.

Buses, maxi-taxis and route taxis

Public transport provision is plentiful, if a little confusing at first. Some buses are operated by the state Public Transport Service Corporation (PTSC), others are privately run.

The government run the large blue and white coaches. PTSC drivers are not allowed to take money so you must buy your ticket before you board. These are available at PTSC terminals, the left luggage terminal at the airport, or selected village shops. The PTSC buses are cheaper than all their competitors but less frequent.

A PTSC Express Commuter Service is being introduced, with limited stops, a quicker travel time, increased comfort but slightly higher fares.

Some sample fares in local currency are given below:

Destination	**TT$**
Piarco Airport to Port of Spain	1.50
Port of Spain to Blanchisseuse	2.25
Port of Spain to Chaguaramas	1.00
Port of Spain to Arima	1.50
Port of Spain to Sangre Grande	2.75
Port of Spain to San Fernando	3.00
San Fernando to Point Fortin	1.50
San Fernando to Mayaro	1.50
San Fernando to Erin	1.50
Sangre Grande to Mayaro	1.50
Point Fortin to Icacos	1.50

The PTSC offices are in South Quay, the old railway station. Ring 623 2341 for information on services. On some routes the buses are several hours apart, others may be half hourly. The airport bus, for example, leaves every hour, on the hour starting at 0500 and ending at 2200. An increased frequency of service is promised, as part of the plan to upgrade the island's infrastructure. Where the PTSC does not go the privately-owned transport does.

Maxi-taxis are minibuses grouped into associations which have a different coloured stripe painted along them. They go when full between two set destinations and offer a frequent service. Maxi-taxis cover many of the routes around Port of Spain, see under 'Port of Spain' for more details.

Route-taxis are more expensive than the PTSC or Maxi-taxis, but still excellent value by any standard. They are saloon cars converted to taxis, with 'H' as the first letter on their numberplates. Unlike private taxis they try to run full and travel fixed routes. The drivers tout for business by honking their horns or gesturing with their free hand. Route-taxis cover the suburbs of Port of Spain, compete on the popular routes for passengers and fill in the gaps in the island's transport system so that you can catch a ride to virtually every village on Trinidad.

Some sample fares in local currency:

Destination	TT$: Maxi-taxi	Route-taxi
Port of Spain to San Fernando	5	10
San Fernando to Point Fortin	5	7
Port of Spain to St Anne	-	2
Port of Spain to Maraval	1.50	2
Port of Spain to St James	1.50	2
Maraval to St James	-	2
Sangre Grande to Toco	-	7

Some hotels offer to pick guests up from the airport; check to see if yours offers this service.

Ferry

Apart from the Trinidad and Tobago service there is one linking Gaspar Grande (also known as Fantasy Island), with Trinidad.

Accommodation

For hotel costs refer to the foreword 'Getting the best out of this guidebook.'

Port of Spain

Top

Trinidad Hilton (Lady Young Road, PO Box 442, tel. 624 3211). One of the world's best sited hotels, it perches on a hill overlooking the Savannah, giving most of the 412 rooms sweeping views of the capital. It has been dubbed the 'upside down hotel' due to the way you enter the lobby at the crest of the hill then descend by elevator to your room. It is owned by the government but managed by Hilton International.

The Hilton attracts a large number of business travellers because of its convention services, telecommunications and interpreters. It has also become part of the island's social scene. Special food festivals are frequently arranged in the Pool Terrace Garden or Boucan restaurants, musical evenings take place in one of three bars.

On site are two tennis courts, badminton, table tennis, shuffleboard, a range of concessionary shops and a 25-metre swimming pool. The hotel is hoping to open a gym and sauna in the near future. All rooms have just been renovated, they come with satellite TV, air-conditioning, mini-bar, balcony and private bar. There are two rooms especially designed for the handicapped and ramp access throughout.

A great place to stay if momey is no object. AMEX, MC, V.

High

Holiday Inn (Wrightson Road, PO Box 1017, tel. 625 3361/8). Built to cater for the business traveller this large concrete building dominates the capital's shoreline. Conference and banqueting rooms are on hand along with all modern telecommunications. Each of the 221 rooms comes with air-conditioning, satellite TV and private bath.

Amenities include two restaurants; one, La Ronde, sited on top of the building, revolves, giving views of the city. There are three bars, a swimming pool and health club. Rates increase sharply over Carnival. AMEX, MC, V.

Middle

Hotel Normandie (10 Nook Avenue, St Anns, PO Box 851, tel. 624 1181/4). A family-owned hotel, originally established in the 1930s by French Creoles, also known as St Anne's Village. It is located in a pleasant area near the northern edge of the Savannah. The 56 rooms come in three different categories, all with air-conditioning.

Beside the hotel is the attractively designed 'market' containing a variety of boutiques and the Cafe Trinidad. Other facilities include the La Fantasie restaurant, the 1234 art gallery and a pool. AMEX, MC, V.

Chaconia Inn (106 Saddle Road, Maraval, PO Box 3340, tel. 628 8603/5). Situated outside Port of Spain but on one of the main Maxi-taxi routes. The Chaconia's restaurant specialises in steaks and on

Hanging out with the homeboys, on the streets of Port of Spain. Street language and fashions from the USA and Europe are readily picked up and adapted by teenagers here.

Saturdays in the high season entertainers perform here. All rooms have air-conditioning, telephones and TV; some also have kitchenettes. The Inn has a pool and is only a short distance from Moka Golf Course. AMEX, MC, V.

Kapok (16-18 Cotton Hill, St Clair, tel. 622 6441). The Savannah and Tiki Village restaurants attached to this hotel are highly regarded for their cuisine. The Kapok is located on the edge of the Savannah park; its rooms are spacious and come with en-suite bathroom, telephone and satellite TV. The hotel, run by the efficient Chan family, offers modern telecommunications and a laundry service; downstairs are a shopping mall and small swimming pool. AMEX, MC, V.

Valley View Hotel (67 Ariapita Road, St Anns, tel. 623 3511). This 68-room hotel aims to cater for the business traveller and tourist. The rooms come with telephone, bathroom and satellite TV. The Valley View probably has the best amenities on Trinidad for the sports enthusiast; these include gym and sauna, two squash courts, two floodlit tennis courts and a large swimming pool with waterslide.

On the premises are a ballroom and conference facilities, as well as the Bedrock nightclub. The St Anns' Route-taxis come up as far as the hotel. AMEX, MC, V.

Queen's Park Hotel (5-5A Queen's Park West, tel. 625 1061). Built in 1895, this old-fashioned hotel is currently closed for renovation. Only the bar, which features jazz bands on Saturday nights is open. A front-facing room with a balcony gives a superb view of all the activity on the Savannah. AMEX, MC, V.

Moderate

Monique's (114 Saddle Road, Maraval, tel. 628 3334). This guesthouse comes highly recommended because of the care Mike and Monique Charbonne take over their guests. They have been in business for 15 years and are currently landscaping the hillside above them to provide more space for their guests.

The rooms are spacious, coming complete with telephone and air-conditioning. There is a TV lounge and restaurant. Washing facilities are available and there is an agreement with the Chaconia that guests here can use the pool there.

Monique's is leading the way in this country in providing facilities to the handicapped. The guesthouse has a specially designed room with wide doors, ramps and bar grips. AMEX, MC, V.

Tropical Hotel (6 Rookery Nook Road, Maraval, tel. 622 5815). The Bamboo Room restaurant, a TV lounge and a swimming pool are located on the premises. Formerly the great house of a sugar plantation, it has been converted into this 16-room hotel. The manageress Wendy Smith is looking to create a homely setting. AMEX, MC, V.

Carnetta's (28 Scotland Terrace, Andalusia, Maraval, tel. 628 2732). This is located down the turning opposite Monique's (keep right). A newly-opened guesthouse with four suites all with air-conditioning and private bathrooms. Rates includes full American breakfast. Owned by veteran hoteliers Winston and Carnetta Borrell. BB; no credit cards.

Alicia's House (7 Coblentz Gardens, St Anns, tel. 623 2802). A 13-room guesthouse down a quiet cul-de-sac. The rooms come with air-conditioning and TV; swimming pool and laundry facilities are on the premises. No credit cards.

Five Star Guesthouse (7 French Street, Woodbrook tel. 623 4006). This old colonial house is located between downtown and St James. Kitchenettes and air-conditioning are available. No credit cards.

Budget

Ellen B Hotel (Dundonald Street, tel. 623 5019). Right in the middle of town, this small guesthouse has seven rooms – some air-conditioned, some with fans – and a central bar/lounge area. No credit cards.

Kestours Sports Villa (58 Carlos Street, Woodbrook, tel. 628 4028). Kestours market Trinidad as a sports destination; they arrange tickets, transfers, fixtures, coaches and accommodation. The rooms are built to take teams and contain bunk beds. At US$ 12 US per night it is very competitive; this includes air conditioning, kitchen, maid service, laundry and TV lounge. Up to 34 may be catered for and it is open to families as well as people on a budget. AMEX, MC, V.

Hillcrest Haven (7A Hillcrest Avenue, Cascade, St Anns, tel. 624 1344). Perched dramatically above the valley is this off-beat, 18-room guesthouse. The bedrooms, of varying size, come with shower and electric fans. There are washing facilities, a kitchen for self-catering and a supermarket just down the road. Formerly a meditation centre it has been run by the Latchmans for over ten years. No credit cards.

La Calypso (46 French Street, Woodbrook, tel. 622 4077), is centrally located, cheap and clean. There are self catering facilities and a TV lounge. On the top floor the sun roof gives a good view of the city. Each room has an electric fan and telephone. No credit cards.

YMCA (20 Woodford Street, tel. 627 6386), can offer basic accommodation at the African Church for US$ 10 per night. The rooms are basic and a little dusty; they come with shower and toilet. No credit cards.

YWCA (8A Cipriani Boulevard, tel. 627 6388 or 622 1029). There are eight shared rooms, and customers are usually women coming from rural areas. Amenities include shared bathroom, communal kitchen, TV room and sitting room. The cost is TT$ 10 US per night depending on the size of the room. No credit cards.

Bed and Breakfast Association of Trinidad

Highly recommended for their professionalism and high standards, the Association's members all agree to maintain a certain standard of service. Each home provides breakfast but other meals are by negotiation. All houses visited were extremely friendly. Association members do not take credit cards. Prices range from US$ 15 to US$ 35 per person, per night. To contact the Association directly write to PO Box 3231, Diego Martin Post Office or telephone 637 9329.

One of the fiercest marketing campaigns in the country is the war between the beers, Carib and Stag. This snack bar near Mount Irvine, Tobago, sports Carib's colours – but undoubtedly sells them both!

Here is a selection of properties:

Zollna House (12 Ramlogan Developments, Maraval, tel. 628 3731), has seven rooms available. The owners Barbara and Fred have retired after many years in the hospitality trade to run their own business. Guests are well cared for here; Barbara has been a driving force in the Association for years. Tours and boat cruises can be arranged.

Charmaine Johnson (16 Buller Street, Woodbrook, tel. 628 7553). This is located close to the National Stadium.

ML's (25 Stone Street, tel. 625 3663), is a colonial house in Port of Spain. The owner also has a beach house in South Trinidad.

Ginna's (Velda Richardson, 54 Archer Street, Belmont, tel. 623 3839), is in downtown Port of Spain.

Kouzminsky's (30 Coblentz Avenue, St Anns, tel. 624 4252), lies in a well kept garden. The owner is interested in antiques and local art.

Accommodation elsewhere on Trinidad

Middle

Bel Air (Piarco International Airport, tel. 664 4771). This 56-room hotel is located just a few hundred metres from the arrivals lounge and a complimentary bus will pick you up if you dial 205 on the courtesy phone. The rooms come with air-conditioning and TV; some are poolside. The Bel Air caters for the needs of the transit traveller rather than the holidaymaker. On Saturdays they put on a barbeque and a band. AMEX, MC, V.

Asa Wright Nature Centre and Lodge (PO Bag 10, Port of Spain, tel. 667 4655). (The full range of activities and the attractions of this sight are discussed later in 'excursions'). The cost of accommodation includes room and all meals. There are 20 simply furnished rooms in total, some in the great house and others newly built in the grounds. MAP; no credit cards.

Farrell House (Southern Main Road, Claxton Bay, tel. 659 2230). A 51-room hotel used by business people and holidaymakers. Each room comes with telephone and TV. There is a poolside area and restaurant. AMEX, MC, V.

Moderate

Whispering Palms (4 1/4 milepost, Mayaro-Guayaguayare Road, PO Box 4033, tel. 630 3336). This is located on Mayaro Bay. The house has recently opened and is somewhat of a hybrid between a bed and breakfast and a guesthouse. It is owned and managed by Jean Lanreth-Smith. There are five spacious rooms with ceiling fans and en-suite bathrooms. Facilities include TV lounge, restaurant and changing rooms. BB; MC, V.

Pax Guesthouse (Mount St Benedict, Tunapuna, tel. 662 4084). The solid stone building below the guesthouse appeals not only to those in search of peace, but also to naturalists who come to walk the trails in the area. Facilities include laundry service and TV lounge. The rooms are spartan; electric fans are provided. All meals may be included in the price upon request. A bus runs down to the main road during monastery visiting hours. MAP optional; no credit cards.

Royal Hotel (46-54 Royal Road, San Fernando, tel. 652 3924). The 30 rooms are equipped for self-catering. No credit cards.

TJ's by the Sea (South Trunk Road, La Romain, tel. 657 9278). This 21-room hotel is located up from the beach on the outskirts of San Fernando. No credit cards.

Timberline Nature Resort (41 1st Avenue, Mount Lambert, tel. 638 2263) is dramatically situated on a headland overlooking the northern coast. Cottages and flats are available in a wild and remote location. No credit cards.

Budget

Park Lane Court (Amethyst Drive, El Dorado, Tunapuna, tel. 663 5265). A small guesthouse offering self-catering rooms complete with TV and bathroom. No credit cards.

Queen's Beach Hotel (Mayaro Bay, tel. 630 3583). More of an oil workers' hotel than a place for the tourist, there are 35 rooms plus a bar. No credit cards.

Green Acres Guest House (Mile Post 23, Balandra Bay; no phone). A small and friendly place run by Mr Hugh Lee Pow. Meals are also included in the price. No credit cards.

Bed and Breakfasts elsewhere on Trinidad

Mr and Mrs Lynch (108A Valley View Drive, Maracas Valley, St Joseph, tel. 663 4413). A double room is available in this well designed and beautifully sited house. Excellent hosts and a good location for hikes to the waterfall or into the Northern Range.

Mr and Mrs Cooper (Paradise Hill, Upper Village, Blanchisseuse, tel. 664 3280). Four bedrooms are available in this well kept house. Mrs Cooper is very knowledgeable on life in the village before it was joined by the road to the outside world.

Erline Alexander (143 Pond Street, La Romain, tel. 657 3749). A very pleasant house on the outskirts of San Fernando, it can be reached by taking a route taxi from the Carnegie Free Library in San Fernando. Mrs Alexander is a school teacher by profession.

Mrs Vanessa Archibald (71 Clifton Hill, Point Fortin, tel. 648 2468). A huge house near the Clifton Hill Club. Two double rooms are available with inter-connecting bathroom.

Mrs Louise McKnight (148 Clifton Hill, Point Fortin, tel 648 3727). Four rooms are available here.

Places to eat

This guide is sub-divided into various types of cuisine. Some of the restaurants could easily fit into two or more categories. A cross reference is given at the end of each section.

Elegant dining

La Boucan (Trinidad Hilton, tel. 624 3211). A mural painted by Geoffrey Holder, a renowned local artist dominates the room. The restaurant is named after the old smoke ovens that sailors used to preserve food before a long voyage, hence the word 'buccaneers'. Here they use the kitchen's boucan for a variety of dishes.

Lunch and dinner are served here, except on Sundays when it closes. The emphasis is on quality and variety. On Mondays it is pot pourri evening, a mixture of local and European colonial dishes. Tuesdays and Thursdays the a la carte menu is available. Wednesday is buffet night: a selection of food from the chef's chosen continent. Friday is a seafood buffet, whilst Saturday brings the week to a close with a gala buffet.

An all-inclusive meal will cost between TT$ 65 and TT$ 110 per person. Scruffy dress is not acceptable; reservations are suggested. AMEX, MC, V.

Cafe Savannah (Kapok Hotel, tel. 622 6441). This restaurant has acquired a good reputation over the years. Located on the ground floor it serves lunch on weekdays and dinner from Monday to Saturday.

For starters try the 'pods of pleasure', a blend of crabmeat and spices wrapped in plantain which is then lightly fried. Lobster, either sauteed with herbs and garlic or grilled in lime butter are long-standing favourites. Smart dress expected; a meal will cost between TT$ 40 to TT$ 80. AMEX, MC, V.

See also **Rafters** and **La Ronde** (Holiday Inn) which could easily be included in this section.

Continental

La Ronde (Holiday Inn, tel. 625 3361/8). The only revolving rooftop restaurant in the Caribbean gives a panoramic view of Port of Spain and the Gulf of Paria. A few local dishes are mixed into the a la carte menu. Smart dress. AMEX, MC, V.

Seafood dishes

Rafters (6 Warner Street, Port of Spain, tel. 628 9258), a converted early 1900s old Portuguese storehouse in the heart of the capital. Your hosts are Richard and Paul Mowser. At lunchtimes its buffet attracts members of the business community; on Fridays and Saturdays the bar is a popular meeting point.

The restaurant makes use of the colonial architecture and dimmed lights to create a relaxed atmosphere. On Wednesday, Friday and Saturday evenings a seafood buffet is laid on, at other times there is the choice from the menu. Try the seafood jubilee or shrimp flambeau. A meal will cost between TT$ 50 and TT$ 90. AMEX, MC, V.

La Fantasie (Hotel Normandie, tel. 624 1181). Breakfast, lunch and dinner are served daily. Dining is in the pastel restaurant or on the small terrace in front of it. The menu features a variety of Creole seafood dishes and an occasional vegetarian meal. TT$ 60 to TT$ 100 per person. AMEX, MC, V.

Surf's Country Inn (North Coast Road, Blanchisseuse, tel. 669 2475) is built on a hillside overlooking the sea. It has acquired a good reputation for fresh fish. Open every day from 1000 hours; costs vary from TT$ 35 to TT$ 60. No credit cards.

Seabelle (27 Mucurapo Road, St James, Port of Spain, tel. 622 3594). A small place open from Monday to Saturday, serving lunch and dinner. TT$ 40 to TT$ 80. No credit cards.

Le Poissonier (3A Saddle Road, Maraval, Port of Spain, tel 628 8186). In the Shoppes of Maraval Mall. Prices range from TT$ 20 to TT$ 80. No credit cards

The **Anchorage** could also be included in this category.

Arabic and Middle Eastern food

Ali Baba's (Royal Palm Plaza, Maraval, Port of Spain, tel. 622 5557). This cafe, with Arabic murals, is located upstairs in the mall and overlooks the street. The menu items are on display at the counter; if you are unsure the staff are very happy to explain the ingredients of the dishes. Kebabs, taboulie, houmos, mousaka, kibi (meatballs) and stuffed cabbage rolls are typical, though there are concessions to Trini tastes.

Ali Baba's is open from 1000 to midnight on Mondays to Saturdays, 1600 to 2200 on Sundays. In the Town Centre Mall there is another branch open during working hours. The piped music is usually soca but occasionally some Arabic songs creep in. A meal will cost from TT$ 15 to TT$ 40. No credit cards.

Barbeque and steaks

Roof Garden (Chaconia Hotel, Maraval, tel. 628 8603/5). Though a range of local and international dishes are served here, steaks are the house speciality. It is a spacious restaurant serving breakfast, lunch and dinner. Dinner will come to TT$ 40 to TT$ 100 per head. AMEX, MC, V.

Anchorage (Point Gourde Road, Chaguaramas, tel. 634 4334). This venue is one of Trinidad's most popular nightspots at the weekends; after dining hours it turns into a club. Constructed from wood, the Anchorage looks out over the ocean and back towards Port of Spain. The menu covers a range of seafood and meat dishes, as well as several interesting cocktails and fruit punches. Expect to spend TT$ 40 to TT$ 80. No credit cards.

Swiss Chalet (Long Circular Mall, St James, Port of Spain, tel. 622 0023). A cafe style layout on the second floor of the mall. Open from 1100 to 2100 hours Mondays and Tuesdays, from 1100 to 2200 Wednesdays and Thursdays and from 1100 to 2300 Fridays and Saturdays. Meals are quite cheap; TT$ 15 to TT$ 20 is typical. No credit cards.

Indian

Monsoon (72 Tragarete Road, Port of Spain, tel. 628 7684). It is amazing that in a country where Indian cooking is so popular, there is only one place that sells this type of cuisine. Actually, the Monsoon is a cross between a take-away and a sit down restaurant. This tastefully decorated establishment is on the site of an old rumshop. It is managed by Mr Randy Attin.

The cooking here is very different to the meals in a British-Indian eating place. The curried goat, lamb, crab or chicken is served up with two types of traditional bread: dhalpuri or paratha. There are a number of relishes and chutneys which can also be added to the food. Finally the Guinness ice cream is a weird and wonderful dessert.

The Monsoon is open from 1100 to 2200 on Mondays to Saturdays. A meal will cost from TT$ 10 to TT$ 50. AMEX, MC, V.

Creole and local cooking

The Veranda (13 Rust Street, St Clair, Port of Spain, tel. 622 6287) is easy to miss on this quiet street in the capital's suburbs. It is owned and run by Phyllis Viera, who provides a small range of tried and tested favourites; lunches only. There is a small bar and tables inside or on the porch. Expect to pay TT$ 30 to TT$ 45. No credit cards.

Une Cachette (Aqua View Terrace, Dhien's Bay, Carenage, tel. 637 5954). A romantic rendezvous, west from Port of Spain past the yacht club. You must make a reservation if you wish to eat in the restaurant. The bar and lounge are open from Monday to Friday from 1600, or from 1800 over the weekend. A meal here costs from TT$ 20 to TT$ 45. No credit cards.

Olympia (Holiday Inn, Port of Spain, tel. 625 3361/68). A selection of creole and international dishes; open for breakfast, lunch and dinner. TT$ 40 to TT$ 120 per person. AMEX, MC, V.

Le Petit Bourg (Farrell House, Southern Main Road, Claxton Bay, tel. 659 2230). Open every day for all meals. The restaurant has a fine view of the sea. The price will be between TT$ 45 to TT$ 60. AMEX, MC, V.

Coconut Village (Cruise Ship Complex, 1D Wrightson Road, Port of

Spain, tel. 627 2648) is open from 1000 Monday to Saturday and is located right by the shopping centre. It sells a variety of snacks and meals as well as alcoholic drinks. TT$ 25 to TT$ 35 per head. No credit cards.

Italian and local

Chequers (100 Saddle Road, Maraval, Port of Spain, tel. 628 7007). The emphasis is on Creole cooking rather than Italian, but there are a few of the latter on the menu. It is open from Monday to Saturday for dinners and weekdays for lunches. There are plans afoot to turn Wednesdays into a members-only club. Lunch is served from 1130 till 1430, dinner from 1900 to 2300. The pumpkin soup is very tasty and if you feel like a drink try the house speciality, a brainstormer, with vodka, white rum, bitters and various fruits. A full meal will cost between TT$ 30 and TT$ 100 per person. AMEX, MC, V.

Chinese and Polynesian delicacies

Tiki Village (Kapok Hotel, tel. 622 6441). The second of the Kapok's enterprising restaurants. Located on the top floor of the building, offering views of the capital. The relaxed atmosphere is made complete by the mini pool and oriental decor. A very popular dining spot so reservations are advised.

There are heaps of mouth-watering dishes to choose from on the menu. Starters include shrimp dumplings or birds nest soup. For the main course try the Hawaiian Luau Fish which is fried in a sweet sauce or the Jar Choi Yuk Pien, pork in a spicy sauce. A selection of vegetarian dishes is available. If you have time, try the Tiki Village at least once. The service charge is discretionary; a meal typically comes to TT$ 45 to TT$ 100. AMEX, MC, V.

Chinese

Hong Kong City (86A Tragarete Road, Newtown, Port of Spain, tel. 622 3949). A newly-opened dining place owned by Pang Chor Yung, where you will be served by his enthusiastic staff. Brightly decorated in red and white oriental carvings, the restaurant has a friendly and informal atmosphere.

The Hong Kong City has a good selection of dishes, the lemon chicken is recommended. Reservations are suggested. It is open from 1100 to 2300 seven days a week.

The upstairs is fitted with a laserdisc karioke system and small stage. A varity of classics, golden oldies and children's nursery rhymes can be played; audience participation is encouraged but not enforced. A meal will total between TT$ 40 and TT$ 80. AMEX, MC, V.

China Palace II (Ellerslie Plaza, Maraval, Port of Spain, tel. 622 5866). This is located upstairs above the shops with a take-away outlet downstairs. Frequently crowded, reservations are advised for evenings over the weekend. A good selection of dishes are on the menu; the service is attentive. The costs will be between TT$ 40 to TT$ 90 per head. AMEX, MC, V.

Soong's Great Wall (97 Circular Road, San Fernando, tel. 652 2583). The most renowned eating place in San Fernando, the place has recently been renovated. Open all week for lunch and for dinners all days except Sunday. Expect to pay TT$ 30 to TT$ 100. No credit cards.

Singho (Long Circular Mall, St James, Port of Spain, tel. 628 2077), located on the second floor of the mall. The decor is oriental, with an aquarium. Pepper shrimps are particularly good here. The cost will be between TT$ 20 to TT$ 60 per head. No credit cards.

New Shay Shay Tien (77-79 Cipriani Boulevard, Port of Spain, tel. 627 8185). A popular place with a high standing amongst the capital's diners. A wide selection of dishes is available. The price is between TT$ 25 and TT$ 45. No credit cards.

Lychee Gardens (Upper Level, West Mall, Westmoorings, tel. 637 2668). A pleasant eating place offering lunch and dinner. You will pay between TT$ 15 and TT$ 80. No credit cards.

Kenny Wong (18 Eastern Main Road, Tunapuna, tel. 645 3169). Open for breakfast, lunch and dinner on Mondays through to Saturdays. The cost is between TT$ 20 and TT$ 60.

Pagoda (59 Independence Avenue, San Fernando, tel. 657 6375). Open from Monday till Saturday for lunch and dinner. It will cost between TT$ 15 and TT$ 50. No credit cards.

Mexican

El Dorado (Ellerslie Plaza, Maraval, Port of Spain, tel. 628 2267). A wide range of Mexican and Venezuelan snacks are available from this small snack bar. Mexican rural scenes and sombrero-wearing staff are moves towards creating the right atmosphere. A meal here will cost from TT$ 10 to TT$ 30. No credit cards.

Vegetarian and local dishes

Veni Mange 13 Lucknow Street, St James, Port of Spain, (no telephone). Owned and run by two of the island's best known personalities, Allyson Hennesy a TV presenter and Rosemary

Hezekiah a jewellery designer. This is where you will taste some of the best Trini cooking served up in large portions, and as Rosemary is a vegetarian, non meat courses are guaranteed.

Take care you do not walk past, there is only a small sign on the wall. Veni Mange is a small colonial house, tastefully decorated with prints of bygone days. It is open for lunch during the weekdays only from 1130 to 1430, though on Friday there is an all afternoon 'lime' at the bar which can go on till 2100. Due to its constant popularity, try to get here early, as reservations are difficult. A meal here will cost TT$ 40 to TT$ 70. No credit cards.

Cascadu (108 Picton Street, Newtown, Port of Spain, tel. 628 5727) is open for lunch on weekdays from 1100 till 1500. Take-aways are also available. It costs TT$ 20 to TT$ 35 per head. No credit cards.

See also **Tiki Village,** the **Hott Shoppe** and **La Fantasie**.

English-Trini

The Pelican Inn (2-4 Coblentz Avenue, tel. 624 7486). Known primarily for its evening entertainment, the Pelican also has a good reputation for business lunches during the week. Mainly local dishes in this pub with an English feel to it. Pay between TT$ 30 and TT$ 60. AMEX, MC, V.

Customised rotis

The Hott Shoppe (Mucurapo Street). 'We didn't invent the roti, we merely perfected the art', is the motto here. Every conceivable combination of this nation's favourite snack is available. Meats could be chicken, beef, goat or shrimp. For vegetables there are pumpkin, potato, chick peas or bodi (string beans). Choose the concoction you want. It is mainly take-away but there are a few stools. The Hott Shoppe is open from Monday to Saturday 1000 to 2200. The cost can vary between TT$ 10 and TT$ 30. No credit cards.

Cake shops and bakeries

La Maison Rustique (16 Rust Street, St Clair, tel. 622 1512). Tea, cakes and biscuits are served in this traditional house. Open from 1000 till 1900 in the week, 1400 till 1900 on Saturdays. The cost is around TT$ 20. No credit cards.

Bread Basket (St Anns Road, Port of Spain, tel. 623 0916). A small bakery, just down from the Normandie. It is open from 0900 to 1800 on weekdays and sells a tasty range of cakes, pies, sandwiches and pizzas. No credit cards.

Fast food

With the West Indian passion for chicken there are Colonel Saunder's everyhere. In heated competition come the other chains: Marios, Pizza Boys/Burger Boys and Royal Castle. Here are some of the main ones:

Pizzeria

Downtown PoS	**Mario's,** Cipriani Boulevard, or 27 Phillip Street.
	Pizza Boys/Burger Boys, 27 Frederick Street.
St James	**Mario's,** Long Circular Mall.
Maraval	**Pizza Boys/Burger Boys,** Ellerslie Plaza.
San Fernando	**Pizza-Pizza,** Montano Plaza, St James Street.
St Augustine	**Mario's,** St Augustine Shopping Plaza.
Chaguanas	**Mario's,** Mid Centre Mall.

Burgers

Downtown PoS	**Royal Castle,** 49 Frederick Street, or 17 Henry Street.
San Fernando	**Royal Castle**, 120 High Street.

Fried chicken

Downtown PoS	**Kentucky Fried Chicken,** 53 Independance Square, or 36 Henry Street.
St James	**Kentucky Fried Chicken**, Romeo Street. and Western Main Road.
Maraval	**Kentucky Fried Chicken**, 89 Long Circular Road.
San Fernando	**Kentucky Fried Chicken**, Coffee Street.

Basics

Banks

Opening hours are from 0800 or 0900 to 1400 on Monday through Thursday. On Friday they are open from 0800 or 0900 till 1200 then again in the afternoon from 1500 to 1700. The smaller branches in remote areas may have more restricted opening hours. All the main banks have branches downtown including Republic Bank (formerly Barclays), (tel. 623 7233), Royal Bank of Trinidad and Tobago, (tel. 625 3511), National Commercial Bank of Trinidad and Tobago, (tel. 625 2893), Bank of Commerce (tel. 627 9325) and the Citibank, (tel. 625 1046/9).

Communications

The Main Post Office (tel. 625 2893), is located on Wrightson Road near the cruise ship complex. It is open from 0700 till 1700. There are branches throughout the country.

International communications links with Trinidad have improved dramatically over the last few years, due to substantial investments being made in the Telecommunications Services of Trinidad and Tobago (TSTT). Most hotels can make international calls and all the main ones have fax machines.

Calls, cables and telexes can be made from the Textel office on Independence Square, which is open round the clock.

For internal calls there are many call boxes all over the island; keep some quarters handy if you intend to use them.

Emergency services

Police: call 990 for immediate assistance. To report an incident contact the nearest station:

Port of Spain, tel. 625 1261.
San Fernando, tel. 652 2561.
Arima, tel. 664 3563.
Sangre Grande, tel. 668 2444.

Fire Department: call 990.
Ambulance: call 990.

Libraries

The central library is located on the northern end of Woodford Square. Outside, the day's newspaper is posted up on the notice board. Inside there is a modest collection of books and public information displays, including one which gives all the hurricane shelters.

On Norfolk Street just off from Charlotte Street and opposite the General Hospital is the reference library. This is probably the best place to come to if you want specific information about the country's history or its wildlife.

Medical

For an ambulance call 990. There are plenty of pharmacies around the country. Trinidad has two main hospitals, Port of Spain General on Charlotte Street (tel. 623 2951), and another out of the city at Mount Hope (tel. 662 7153). There are dental practices and opticians in the larger settlements.

Newspapers

The nation has two dailies: the *Trinidad Guardian* which is the oldest, editorially independent paper and the *Trinidad and Tobago Express* which tends to take a pro-government line. There are a number of sensationalist weekly rags of the 'man attacked by mutant sprout' variety if you require some light reading, the most famous of which is *The Bomb*.

Foreign papers are available in the better newsagents in Port of Spain but are expensive.

Places of worship

Most of the major world religions are represented in Trinidad. Many people are deeply religious yet very tolerant of the beliefs of others. There is a huge variety of different Christian denominations, though the Catholic church has traditionally had the largest following. Religious centres are shown below:

Denomination	Church	Address	Time of service
Anglican	All Saints	13 Queens, Park West, PoS.	0730 and 1800 Sunday.
Baha'i		Baha'i meeting, Petra Street, PoS.	0800 Sunday.
Buddhist		Methuen Street, Woodbrook, PoS.	1000 Sunday.
Hindu	Mandir	Ethel Street, St James.	1800 Sunday.
Methodist	Hanover Church	Duke Street, PoS.	0900, 1800 Sunday.
Moslem	Sunnat-Ul-Jamaat Assoc.	2 Queen Street, PoS.	five times daily.
Pentecostal	Pentecostal Cathedral,	29-31 Duke Street, PoS.	1830 Sunday.
Presbyterian	Church of Scotland,	50 Frederick Street, PoS.	0800 Sunday.
Roman Catholic	Immaculate Conception,	Independence Square, PoS.	0900 Sunday.

Tourist information

There is a tourist information desk at the airport, from here you may contact hotels if you do not have a booking. The main offices of the Tourism Development Authority are at 134-138 Frederick Street (tel.

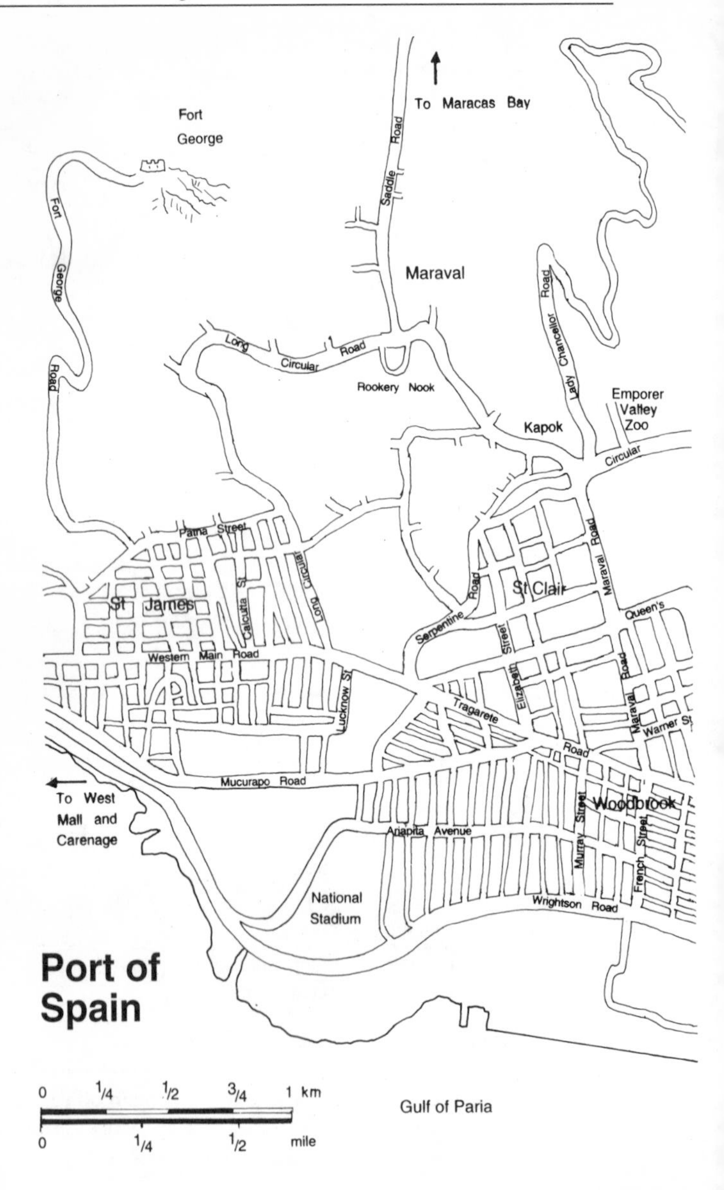
To Maracas Bay
Fort George
Saddle Road
Fort George Road
Maraval
Lady Chancellor Road
Long Circular Road
Rookery Nook
Emporer Valley Zoo
Kapok
Circular
Patna Street
Calcutta St
Long Circular
St James
St Clair
Maraval Road
Serpentine Road
Queen's
Elizabeth Street
Western Main Road
Lucknow St
Tragarete Road
Maraval Road
Warner St
Mucurapo Road
To West Mall and Carenage
Woodbrook
Murray Street
French Street
Ariapita Avenue
National Stadium
Wrightson Road
Port of Spain
0 1/4 1/2 3/4 1 km
0 1/4 1/2 mile
Gulf of Paria

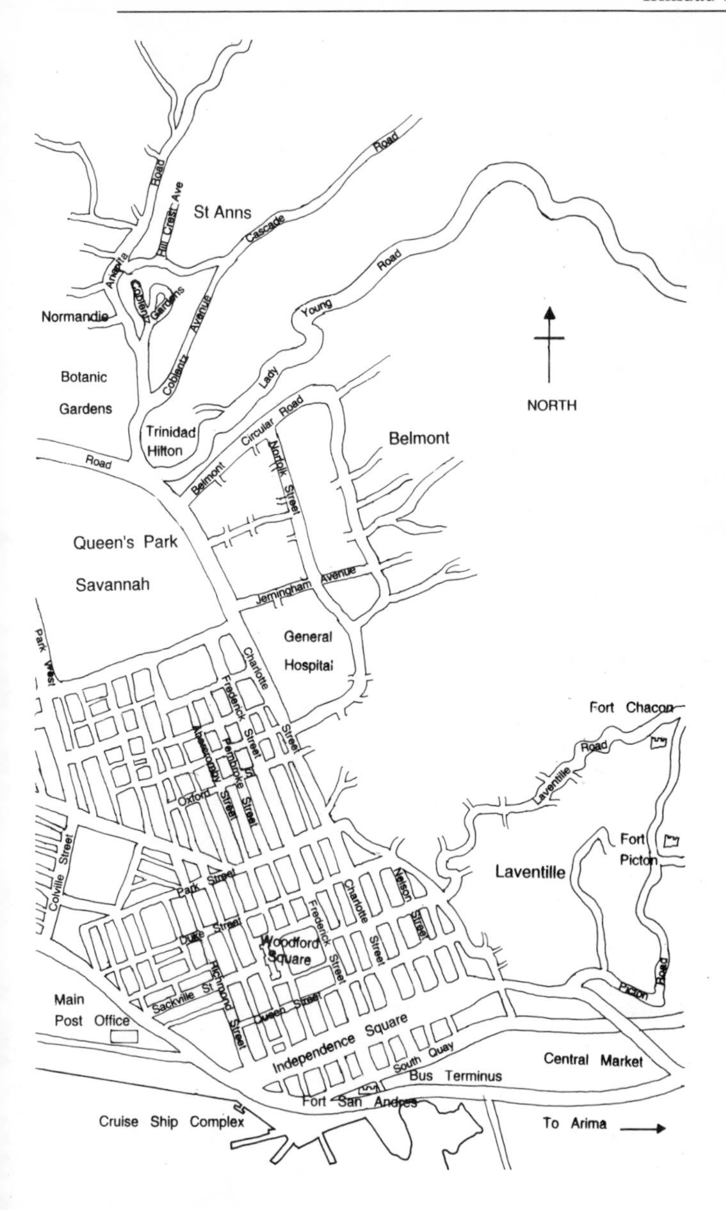
Road
St Anns
Hill Crest Ave
Cascade
Road
Young
Road
Lady
Normandie
Coblentz Gardens
Avenue
Coblentz
Botanic
Gardens
Trinidad
Hilton
Road
Belmont
Circular
Road
Norfolk
Street
NORTH
Belmont
Queen's Park
Savannah
Jerningham
Avenue
General
Hospital
Park West
Charlotte
Street
Frederick
Street
Pembroke
Street
Oxford
Street
Fort Chacon
Road
Laventille
Fort
Picton
Laventille
Colville
Street
Park
Street
Nelson
Street
Charlotte
Street
Frederick
Street
Duke
Street
Woodford
Square
Richmond
Street
Sackville St
Picton
Road
Main
Post Office
Queen
Street
Independence Square
South Quay
Central Market
Bus Terminus
Fort San Andres
Cruise Ship Complex
To Arima

623 1932/4). In addition to advice they can give you print outs on almost any information you require. Restaurants, nightclubs, sightseeing, car hire, history, folklore, wildlife to name but a few.

The Tourism Development Authority is a helpful and efficient organisation.

The sights of Port of Spain

Port of Spain on the surface does not look a very interesting city. At rush hour the streets are liable to be jammed with traffic, some of the streets look quite shabby and several of the buildings damaged in the 1990 coup have still not been repaired. Furthermore the capital is several miles away from a good beach.

Its redeeming feature is the Savannah, a huge park in its centre. When you take a stroll around here and see the people liming, picnicking, playing football and cricket or out walking and jogging, the place starts to grow on you. The Savannah is Trinidad's place for watching the world go by and as you do, all the negative impressions you have built up seem to seep away.

There was nothing here but a few shacks, thickets and swamps when Governor Moneda decreed in 1757 that Puerto de los Hispanioles would be the capital. It was felt that this coastal area would be healthier than St Joseph further inland. The settlement did not prosper until there was an influx of French colonists in the 1780s. The Rio Santa Ana was diverted to assist the town's growth and Fort Chacon constructed to protect it.

When the British took over more defences were added. Towards the end of the nineteenth century the city's suburbs of Laventille, St James, St Anns and Maraval had begun to sprawl into the surrounding countryside.

Today it is a city with suburbs of wooden Victorian homes, imposing skyscrapers and rows of shacks jumbled up the hillside. Mosques, Hindu temples and churches are all within a few metres of each other as are vegetable markets outside department stores. A quiet city it is not; its bustle matches the liveliness within every Trinidadian.

After walking around the streets to get your first impressions of such a multi-faced city, there are a few places that are especially worth a visit.

The De Luxe Cinema in Port of Spain is only one of many on the island. Trinis are keen movie-goers. Two current, big name movies make up a typical evening's viewing, at a fraction of the price of what a visitor would expect to pay.

Historic buildings of downtown Port of Spain

Rather than there being an old heart of colonial buildings in Port of Spain, those that remain are scattered around the city. A series of fires have destroyed many of them.

Independence Square in the centre of the city was laid out in 1816 and it went from being King Street to Marine Square before receiving its current name. Today the country's Treasury building, several banks and the imposing twin towers of the **Financial Complex** are situated here. This TT$ 400-million building is 22 storeys high, earthquake proof and decorated with murals and carvings by local artists.

The sea used to come up to the southern edge of Independence Square, now the Broadway, which on this side leads down to the bus terminal, formerly the old railway station. Just down from here stands **Fort St Andres** and its battery of guns. The fort is unusual in not having the thick walls and narrow windows normally associated with military architecture. It is occupied by the traffic police at the moment and currently under renovation.

Dominating the eastern end stands the Roman Catholic **Cathedral of the Immaculate Conception**. Even though they were Anglican the British authorities encouraged its construction as a gesture to the mainly French-speaking Catholic inhabitants.

The Cathedral is made from blue metal stone from the nearby hills. Many of the furnishings were imported from Europe and the first service was held in 1832. More recent additions have included Irish stained glass windows and carvings of the stations of the cross. At the far eastern end of Independence Square is a statue of Christopher Columbus, the island's first European arrival.

The centre of the Square has been turned into the **Drag** which is a collection of stalls selling tapes, crafts and snacks. They have become squats and their scruffy, downbeat appearance is in marked contrast to the gleaming surfaces of the twin towers. At one of the junctions is a statue of one of the nation's early heroes, Arthur Cipriani, a City Mayor and long-standing critic of colonial administration.

The western end of the square opens out onto the Port Authority; every day the Tobago ferry departs from here. Beside the harbour is the cruise ship complex and its shopping mall; further down is the Main Post Office.

Frederick Street is the main shopping area where department stores and malls lead off from both sides and banners draped across the road indicate a sale at this stall or that. Soon the left side opens up into **Woodford Square**, named after one of the more industrious and successful governors. In 1808 gallows were erected to hang the leaders of a failed slave rebellion. Due to its position opposite the Red House, the seat of government, it has long been the rallying place for popular protest. In 1956 it was dubbed the 'University of Woodford' Square as Dr Eric Williams made many of his campaign speeches from here. In 1970 the tables were turned on him when the Black Power leaders rallied in the square to lambast his government, renaming the park the 'People's Parliament'. Nowadays its uses are purely recreational; it is often the venue for concerts on national holidays.

The Red House: the present building dates from 1907 as its predecessor was destroyed in rioting over the increase in water rates in 1903. The Governor narrowly escaped with his life and 18 people died when the police fired into the crowd to break them up. Parts of the building are open to the public.

In 1990 the entire building was taken over by the Muslimeen in

Trini speak

Here are a few of the sayings you may commonly meet during your stay:

Bacchanal a noisy event, a din, a party or noisy quarrelling.

'Beewee' the affectionate term for BWIA the national airline.

Buffing the act of telling someone off.

Canboulay a march through the streets with lighted torches to celebrate the burning of the cane after the harvest.

Fetes (pronounced fett). You do not go to parties here, you go to fetes, the same things happen but the name is different.

Jour Ouvert the opening day of the Carnival.

Liming more of an art than a word, this is what most Trinis live for. Liming is hanging around with friends, it could be partying, socialising, chatting or just watching the world go by. It is the art of relaxing and having a good time. Most of the people have degrees in liming.

Macko (phonetic), someone who is macocious, in other words they make mischief, gossip, badmouth people and involve themselves in others' business.

Pan steel band music.

Panyard where a steel band meets to practice.

Play mas the act of joining a band for the Carnival. It involves buying the band's costume, following it in procession and giving them your allegiance in the marches and competitions. The tourist office have details of how visitors can get involved.

Sous sous a system traditionally used for saving money, it derives from the French word sous – a small coin. Every member of the group puts in an equal sum over a period of months equal to the number of people involved. Each month all draw lots, the winner takes all that sum to spend and is precluded from future draws.

Wine the most popular type of dancing – from the hips.

Winer girl a dancer who gyrates her body irresistibly.

their ill-fated bid for power. Most of the government were captured and held hostage for six days, whilst security men were murdered as the building was stormed. The damage has been repaired and a monument erected to remember the days when the country's future hung in the balance.

Trinity Anglican Cathedral faces Woodford Square's southern side. It was begun in 1816. The ceiling is copied from Westminster Hall and supported by mahogany beams. Governor Woodford's statue stands inside.

Historic Buildings around the Savannah

The **National Museum and Art Gallery** (tel. 623 6419), at the junction of Frederick and Keate Street was built in 1923 on the site of a science and art museum which was destroyed by fire. It is open from 1000 till 1800 Tuesdays to Saturdays. Entrance is free but you will be required to leave all bags and camera equipment with the attendant at the door.

The ground floor has exhibits on the geology of both islands including quirks like the Pitch Lake. There are displays on the Amerindians and the history of the islands. The development of the oil industry is covered followed by a large display of Carnival costumes. Upstairs is devoted to displays of sculpture, prints and paintings of local artists, apart from a wing showing the wildlife of Trinidad and Tobago. Beside the museum is the cenotaph for members of the armed forces who died during both world wars.

The **Magnificent Seven** are a remarkable collection of buildings that edge onto the Savannah; all are unique architecturally. With one exception they were all built in 1904 when the plantation owners were enjoying a period of great prosperity. All are in private or public hands and are not open to visitors. A mark of how importantly the government values its heritage is that all buildings in public hands have been restored or are going through the process.

Beginning with the southernmost building, there is **Queen's Royal College** which is now a boy's secondary school. This is constructed from concrete in a mock-German Renaissance style. Famous pupils have included VS Naipaul and Dr Eric Williams.

Hayes Court is the residence of the Anglican Bishop of Trinidad. Incorporating a blend of French and British influences, it was built later than the others, in 1910.

Mille Fleurs A grand house decorated with fretwork, it is now being used as a government office.

Ambard House or **Roomor** is a mixture of French and Italian influences. Its roof is a collection of towers, spires and galleries. It is privately owned.

Archbishop's House is the official residence of the Roman Catholic Bishop of Port of Spain. Its design uses marble and granite brought over from Ireland, and shows Italian influences.

Whitehall This building, built in a Venetian style, was requisitioned by the US military during the war. It is now the Prime Minister's Office.

Killarney is in many ways the most remarkable and outlandish. Its design was said to be inspired by Balmoral Castle in Scotland and is constructed of brick and limestone. Its turrets and spires conjure up images of Count Dracula's Retreat, rather than a plantation house. The Stollmeyer family sold it to the government and it now houses their offices.

Other interesting buildings around the Savannah are the **Queen's Park Hotel** of 1895, currently closed for renovation, **Knowsley**, another great house, now a government office and **All Saints Church** which was constructed in 1846.

The **Savannah** was bought by the city in 1817. It is a huge recreational park, where people come to stroll and jog. Football and rugby is played here in season. At the southern end of the park is the racetrack and Grandstand. There have been meetings here since the 1820s. At the northern end of the Savannah are some shallow ponds edged with flower beds.

Over the road to the north are the **Botanic Gardens** which were laid out by David Lockhart in 1820. They surround the official residence of the President of the Republic which was built in an L-shape design in 1875.

The gardens contain a huge collection of plants in what is the oldest collection of its kind in the Western hemisphere, including many species from South America and Africa. It is a popular meeting place amongst Trinidadians at the weekend. A lot of care is taken in maintaining the gardens, ensuring most of the shrubs and trees are labelled.

Emperor Valley Zoo (tel. 622 3530), opened in 1952 and is billed as one of the best collections of animals in the Caribbean; including fish, primates, reptiles, birds and amphibians. In all there are 2,000 specimens on eight acres of land. The staff try to keep the animals in surroundings that resemble their natural habitat as much as possible. Several species have been successfully bred in captivity. The zoo is open all week from 0930 till 1700. Entrance costs TT$ 3 for adults and TT$ 1.50 for children of three to 12 years of age.

Around this area there are lots of vendors selling ice creams and soft drinks from push carts.

By taking Lady Road at the foot of the Hilton you come to **the Lookout**, which gives excellent views of the city.

The outlying Forts

Fort Picton perches on a shoulder of land overlooking Laventille, one of the poorer suburbs. The fort was built by the first British governor and is named after him. It was constructed at the time the British were expecting a counter-attack by the Spanish and when most of the population had been alienated by the governor's bloody methods.

The fort is built like the martello towers found in the Channel Islands, with small loopholes and thick walls. Its interior is not accessible; however, you may walk around the fort at any time. The Tourism Development Authority have erected a plaque giving information on its history.

Fort Chacon was built by the last Spanish governor in an attempt to deter attackers. It is also above Laventille, a few hundred yards from Fort Picton. It is smaller and in a ruined state. The remains are fenced off and used as a police wireless station.

Fort George is the most impressive of the nation's defences, both in terms of its location and the extent of its fortifications. It was begun in 1805 during the Napoleonic War. Later it was extended to include a signal station which was designed by Prince Kofi Nti, an Ashanti prince who was in exile.

The fort has been restored to its former state; it features rows of cannon, the gunpowder storerooms and a small museum. Perhaps best of all are the excellent views: of Port of Spain, down the islands westward, or south towards central Trinidad.

Fort George is reached from St James. First turn off Western Main Road onto George Cabral Street, then down Fort George Road. It is open from 1000 till 1800; admission is free. It is difficult to get to unless you have your own transport as it is a long way up from St James and very few people use the road except at weekends.

Art Galleries

It was Jean Michel Cazabon who put the country onto the artistic map. He was born in 1813, went abroad to study then came back to Trinidad to paint a series of landscape watercolours which were widely admired and left an impressive record of life in the mid-to-late nineteenth century. Cazabon died in 1888. Nowadays his prints are widely available – mounted or unmounted in souvenir shops.

Internationally-known contemporary artists include Ralph and Vera Baney, Carlisle Chang, Leroy Clarke, Dermot Lousion and Nina Squires. The current art scene revolves around three art galleries:

Opposite: *Fruit stalls similar to this are a common sight in all the towns and villages around Trinidad. Fresh fruit is a lot cheaper here than on neighbouring islands.*

ON THE ROAD TO ITALY!
APPLES
4 for

Aquarela Galleries, 1A Dere Street, Port of Spain, (tel. 625 5982).
Art Creators, Flat 402, Aldegonda, 7 St Anns Road, Port of Spain, (tel. 624 4369).
Mark Perreira, 101 Tragerete Road, Woodbrook, Port of Spain.

Nightlife

The vibrant nightlife is one of the biggest attractions of Trinidad; there is always so much to choose from, be it a show, or concert, bar or nightclub. Things go on till very late here.

Theatres

There are three theatres in Port of Spain and one in San Fernando; performances are well covered in the newspapers. **The Queen's Hall** (tel. 624 1284), is on St Anns Road near the Hilton, the **Little Carib** (tel. 622 4644), is on the junction of White and Roberts Streets whilst the **Central Bank Auditorium** (tel. 625 4835/5028), is part of the Twin Towers financial complex. The entrance to this theatre is through Eric Williams Plaza.

Cinemas

This is an island of keen movie goers. There are over a dozen cinemas in the main settlements. Here it is usual for a feature to include two major films – around four hours of entertainment. One of these sittings will cost between TT$ 7 to TT$ 10, depending on the seat.

Steel bands

Amoco Renegades Panyard Charlotte Street, Port of Spain, is on the left just down the hill from the hospital. The place where this famous band come together to practice is now open to the public and is literally just an open yard. The band perform every Friday from about 2100 till 0100. Entrance is free, just stroll in.

Opposite, top: *Children out on parade on Emancipation Day, a national holiday celebrating the end of slavery. It is marked by processions and an outdoor concert in Port of Spain.*

Opposite, bottom: *The villagers out bathing on Blanchisseuse beach. On the weekends the coast is a popular 'liming' spot all over Trinidad.*

By going public instead of performing in secret in the run up to Carnival, the Amoco Renegades now make it possible for visitors to see pan music all year round. Most weeks there is guest band or singer, even the great David Rudder has put in an appearance here.

Some rows of seats have been erected, and a bar selling snacks, soft drinks and beers opens on the night. A wide range of people of all ages and from all walks of life come to watch the performance. If you are at all interested in Trini music do not miss this.

Nightclubs

In Trinidad it is often difficult to know the difference between a bar and a nightclub, the distinctions between them easily blur. Some bars have DJ nights when to all intents and purposes they resemble nightclubs. A lot depends on the night you choose to visit.

Anchorage (Point Gourde Road, Chaguaramas, tel. 634 4334). At weekends this restaurant becomes one of the island's most popular nightclubs. The music is a combination of soca, reggae and disco. The Anchorage is no small venue yet it soon gets so full it is difficult to move.

There is a cover charge on the door and scruffily dressed people are unlikely to get in. You pay for drinks with chits which you then take to the bar. The music continues till after 0400. Without a car this place is quite difficult to get to. The busier the place the smarter the dress code.

The Attic (Shoppes of Maraval, Maraval, Port of Spain, tel. 622 8123). This is a small club looking like a ski chalet above the shopping mall. Offering cocktails, snacks and satellite TV as well as a DJ, it bills itself as the 'Dancing Pub'. The music is a mixture of soca and reggae except for 'nostalgia night' on Mondays and Latin evenings on Tuesdays and Thursdays. Dress regulations vary from informal to semi-formal depending on the night. Cover charge.

Upper Level Club (West Mall, Westmoorings, tel. 637 1753). A small club offering a calypso night on Thursdays, which stays open till very late.

Genesis (Starlite Shopping Centre, Diego Martin), attracts a younger crowd. The owners have been criticised for the harshness of their on-the-door policy.

Bedrock at the Valley View Hotel, Ariapita Avenue, Port of Spain. Over the weekends this nightspot features a mixture of live bands, soft rock and western music. The usual cover charge on the door is TT$ 20.

Fifth Avenue (Upper Level, Gulf City, La Romain), on the outskirts of San Fernando. Open from Tuesday to Saturday till 0400; on Fridays it is by invitation only.

The Tunnel (89 Union Road, Marabella, San Fernando, tel. 658 1838). Open from Friday to Sunday till 0400. A bar with dance floor or a place where you can find somewhere to sit and chat, as you prefer.

Club Pizzaz (Gulf City Mall, La Romain, San Fernando, tel. 652 3719). A cocktail lounge and bar; open all week except Mondays. On some nights there is live entertainment; for details call the management.

Fantasy Island (Gasparee Island, tel. 622 1572/4588). Increasingly there are fetes laid on at weekends, with ferries from the mainland, food, and DJs playing through to the early hours of the morning.

Bars

Pelican Inn (2-4 Coblentz Avenue, Port of Spain, tel. 624 7486). This is a long time favourite of locals, expatriots and tourists. One of the oldest bars on the island, the Pelican is done out like an English pub. At lunchtime it is popular for business lunches, whilst in the evenings you can come and enjoy a game of darts.

On Thursday, Friday and Sunday nights there is a cover charge on the door and the place has a resident DJ. At this time the mood changes, it is loud, packed and full of atmosphere.

Valley View Hotel (Ariapita Road, St Anns, Port of Spain, tel. 624 0490). On Friday and Saturday nights a pianist plays in the bar here. For the younger at heart there is the **Bedrock** across the forecourt.

Mas Camp Pub (Ariapita Avenue, Port of Spain, tel. 627 8449), in the centre of the city. This is a lively bar with a succession of live bands or loud music on throughout the week. It gets very crowded at weekends; very much a crowd of locals mixed with a few enterprising visitors.

Wazo Deyzeel (Carib Way, Sydenham Avenue, St Anns, Port of Spain, tel. 623 0115). A cafe/bistro whose owners have tried to create somewhere different to go in the evenings. Seeking a more select crowd and ambiance, the Wazo Deyzeel puts on alternative entertainments such as evenings of poetry reading by local writers.

It is open from 1600 till midnight from Sunday to Thursday, 1200 till 0100 on Fridays and 1600 till 0100 on Saturdays. The Wazo Deyzeel is quite hard to find; it is tucked away off Ariapita road soon after the Hotel Normandie.

Rafters (6A Warner Street, Woodbrook, Port of Spain, tel. 628 9258). In addition to being a locally acclaimed restaurant this is a popular gathering place on Friday and Saturday nights, with the resident DJ playing through till well after midnight.

Moon over Bourbon Street (West Mall, tel. 637 3448), a first floor cafe bistro with a large balcony area. Local artists often gig here, making it a popular meeting place before going on to a nightclub. Open from Wednesday to Sunday from 1700.
Farrell House Hotel (Southern Main Road, Claxton Bay, tel. 659 2230). The bar and restaurant have live entertainment and dancing on Friday nights for those in the south of the island.
The Cricket Wicket (Tragarete Road, St James, Port of Spain). A small bar so-named for its position opposite the Queen's Park Oval cricket ground. Very popular on Friday afternoons with the after-work crowd.
Smokey and Bunty (Western Main Road, St James, Port of Spain). A raucous bar-come-rumshop which opens onto the street in St James; an area which is always lively after dark.
The Jazz Club (Queen's Park Hotel, 5-5A Queen's Park West, Port of Spain, tel. 625 1061). On Saturday nights the Queen's Park Hotel has a jazz band on and the bar stays open, even when the hotel is closed for renovation.
Une Cachette (Dheine's Bay, Chaguaramas, tel. 637 5954). In addition to serving meals this nightspot also lays on DJs and music on most days of the week.
Half Moon Pub (34A Bossiere Village, Maraval, Port of Spain). A local watering hole with pool, darts and snacks available on the premises.

As venues can change their evening entertainments quite regularly, it is suggested you call ahead to confirm any activities available.

The sights of San Fernando

Trinidad's second and only other city is San Fernando, whose population is now over 60,000. For decades a small village existed here but growth did not really take off till after the harbour was opened. The town became a municipality in 1845, a borough in 1853 and finally, over a century later in 1988, it was designated a city. Most of Trinidad's industrial strength is in the south and San Fernando is at the centre of it.

The oddly-shaped San Fernando hill dominates the surrounding area. It is 195 metres high and 26 hectares in size. It might not have existed today if it had not been for the actions of some of the city's residents. Over the years quarries have extracted gravel from it and

only after complaints from the citizens was this finally stopped. It is now a recreation area; a road leads up to the top allowing people to enjoy the views of central Trinidad.

As early as 8000 BC the hill featured in Amerindian legends. The area was occupied by the Warao and Gwaraunos who made it a sacred place naming it 'Anaparima', or the World Mountain. This was the final resting place of Haburi the hero and his mother who were fleeing from the Frog Woman. On reaching safety on Trinidad they were turned into 'Anaparima'. Thereafter it became a place of pilgrimage.

In 1784 the last Spanish Governor, Don Chacon, named the place San Fernando de Naparima, the only place in the country to be named by royal decree. With such a mouthful to contend with, the latter part of the name was gradually lost. Sometimes the city is abbreviated even further, down to 'Sando'.

The downtown area

On Carib Street at the foot of the hill is the oldest house in the city, having been built in 1833. Carib Street leads into the centre of town. Here stands the **Carnegie Free Library** which was opened in 1919.

Slow train coming

In the 1800s it was the great merchants and plantation owners of Trinidad who supplied the impetus for development when there was inaction from the colonial administration. So it was with the coming of the railways.

The first line from Princes Town to San Fernando was little more than a tramway; the track was laid in 1859. Waggons were drawn along it by horses and mules and carried agricultural produce to the coast. Then by popular demand the service was extended to carry passengers and mail. It became known as 'the Cipero Tramroad' after the river it crossed; the fare was 36 cents.

The idea of a railway proper had been around since 1846 when the Trinidad Railway Company was formed. Routes were surveyed, yet it proved impossible to raise the finance until the Cipero Tramroad had shown the way.

In 1873 construction began and on 31 August 1876 a line linking Port of Spain with Arima opened. A mini railway mania hit the country as people of influence clamoured to have a branch put through to their own town or estates. In 1882 San Fernando was reached; in 1897 the network had been expanded to take in Sangre Grande, Tabaquite, Siparia and Rio Claro.

The service ran successfully for decades then after independence, the government started to have misgivings about it and lines were gradually closed down. The final run to San Fernando from Port of Spain was a memorable event; people struggled to get a place on board, Calypsonians sang of the railway's demise. The final track was pulled up in 1968; in some places roads were laid along the old routes.

Little remains today: Engine 11 stands in San Fernando's Harris Promenade, whilst its sister locomotive occupies a corner of the bus depot in Port of Spain. The capital's railway station is now the headquarters of the Public Transport Service Corporation. All are monuments of this bygone age.

Was it the right thing to do? With the oil boom the roads are now packed with cars clogging up the cities and belching exhaust fumes into the air. At times you hear regret at the passing of the railways, but it is unlikely that Trinidadians will ever hear the locomotives whistle again.

The Scottish benefactor Andrew Carnegie gave enough money to allow the construction to begin. In 1984 its books were destroyed by fire.

The main area of historical interest is the **Harris Promenade** off High Street. This was so-named after Lord Harris, one of the

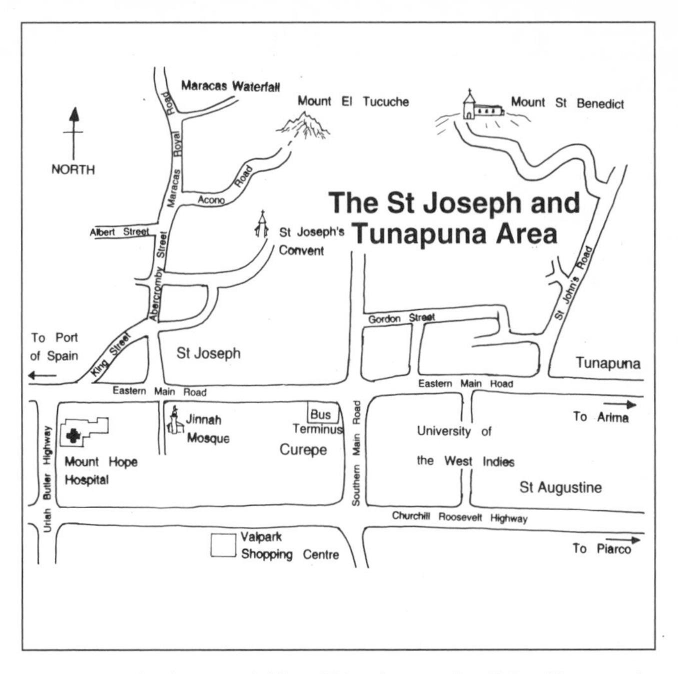

governors who interested himself in the town's affairs. He gave the Promenade to the local council who built their town hall here. On the square is a statue of Mahatma Gandhi which was erected in 1952.

The small locomotive that rests here is symbolically '**the Last Train**', in other words the locomotive that made the final journey before the tracks were pulled up. Engine Number 11 is squat and brightly painted, it sits on the gravel quietly rusting away.

At the other end of the square is San Fernando General Hospital and the law courts. Nearby is the Naparima Bowl, a recreational centre.

If you walk down the hill along High Street you will come to the bus station and the waterfront, an area of much bustle and queueing. All the city's modern development is taking place in the suburbs with the construction of flashy new shopping malls like the one at Gulf City.

Touring the countryside

Out west towards Chaguaramas

Travelling out this way is known locally as going 'down the islands'. The government has set up a Development Authority to attract investment to this area.

Take the Western Main Road out of Port of Spain. The first village reached is Carenage, the home of the Anchorage restaurant and nightclub. Next comes the larger settlement of Chaguaramas. The Convention Centre is on the right and the heliport is on the left. This is now the area of the old US base. The massive hangars and warehouses give an impression of just how large the facilities were. Many of the buildings are now used as a base by the Trinidad and Tobago Defence Force.

The Yachting Association are based here and there is the beach down at Chagville, though this is not as impressive as the bays elsewhere. **Hart's Cut** was opened here in 1856 allowing fishing boats to take a short cut and avoid the headland. **Staubles Bay** is the home of the Trinidad and Tobago Coastguard.

After Chaguaramas if you turn right up Tucker Valley you come to **Macqueripe** with its sandy bay. On this section of coast stands an old wartime tracking station. Another good place to pause is **Scotland Bay** at the end of the peninsular.

Of all the islands the most developed is **Gasparee**, which is also known as Gaspar Grande and Fantasy Island just to confuse matters. There used to be two old whaling stations here; now it's the home of the very affluent. There have been attempts to develop the island as a tourist resort but for the moment it is being used as a weekend venue for large organised parties.

The **Gasparee Caves** are one attraction; they are entered by stairs from Point Baleine. Inside are stalactites and stalagmites; the water level in the caves changes with the tides. Above the caves are a pair of World War II artillery pieces. Nearby are a few islets. One, Creteau, is a quarry; the other, Carrera is a high security prison.

Two other islands are of interest. **Monos** is an island of rich homes, well known for its fishing. The furthermost island is **Chacachacare** or 'Chaca'. To the west of here are the waters of the Dragon's Mouth and then Venezuela. In 1877 a leper colony was established here, it closed after the war but the buildings remain. Patrick Leigh Fermor describes visiting it in *The Traveller's Tree*.

The northern coast

By taking the Saddle Road through Maraval you can head to the beaches of the north coast, the best on the island. The road follows the coast till Blanchisseuse when it turns south and crosses the Northern Range, passing the Asa Wright Nature Centre and coming down to Arima. It is then easy to return to the capital via the Eastern Main Road.

The drive down to Maracas Bay must be one of the most dramatic in the Caribbean. After a steady climb into the rainforest you begin to descend. As the road hugs the hillside, glimpses of the ocean can be made out far below. Take advantage of the stopping points on the way down as the views are magnificent.

Maracas Bay is a magnificent stretch of beach. The waves are strong and the current can be fierce; it's often good for surfing but take care, watch the flags put out by the lifeguard. At weekends thousands of Trinis come down to the beach to party. People come to the same place each week so they can rendezvous with their friends. Stalls sell beers, soft drinks or shark and bake, the snack everyone on this beach eats. There are plenty of beach facilities provided including changing rooms and showers.

Las Cuevas Bay is the next inlet as you head eastwards, another 8 kilometres (5 miles) further on. Not as popular as Maracas but still full of life and with similar amenities. Further out an offshore rock is emblazoned with the word 'Hollyweed'; I wonder what that could mean?

Blanchisseuse is the final village on the coast before heading inland again. Before the road was put through this way it took several days to reach Port of Spain, as the older residents can still remember. Blanchisseuse has changed little, it is still a collection of pastel-coloured cottages. The villagers still earn a livelihood through fishing. There is a store, a couple of rumshops, a post office and a good bed and breakfast.

In Blanchisseuse the road forks; a coastal track to Toco Bay continues along the coast for a few miles then peters out and is impassable after a few miles. The road to Arima takes you through the lush rainforest area. Keep your eyes peeled to see many types of tropical fruit growing wild.

Paria Waterfall, generally regarded as the finest on the island, is reached from this road. At the 12 ½ mile post you turn east and drive 6 ½ kilometres (4 ¾ miles) till you reach Brasso Seco. At the 4 mile post take the trail that leads northwards. Follow this over the Jordan River till you reach the beach. Turning east walk till you come to the bridge, after walking for five minutes along the right bank you will see the waterfall. The walk should take around two hours each way. An alternate approach is along the coastal path.

On your right as you head south to Arima is the **Asa Wright Nature Centre**. This is probably the premier spot for field naturalists. It is boasted that in a week here it is possible to see around half of the 400 species of birds on the island. Visitors may stay in the on-site accommodation or just come for the day.

The Centre began as a plantation in the early 1900s. In 1947 Dr Newcome and Asa Wright bought the place, and being keen naturalists they began to take in guests who wished to study the area. In 1967 after her husband had died, Asa found the estate difficult to manage on her own and sold the property to a trust. The site was later amalgamated with the Simla Research Station which had been operated for a number of years by Dr William Beebe, a world renowned zoologist.

There are guided tours around the centre or out to other places of interest. **Dunston Cave** is one of the prime attractions, as it is the most accessible nesting site of the oilbird. This is the only nocturnal fruit-eating bird in the world, and gets its name from the Amerindians who hunted it for its body oil. Flash photography is allowed in the caves as it does not disturb the birds.

Asa Wright's is open every day of the week from 0900 till 1700. Bookings should be made 48 hours in advance. Admission is US$ 6 for adults and US$ 4 for children under 12 years of age.

Port of Spain's suburbs

The two valleys either side of Port of Spain are of some interest. To the west lies Diego Martin Valley which is reached by turning north at West Mall. On the river of the same name are the **Blue Basin Falls** which are a five-minute walk from the road. The waterfall is small rather than dramatic, and at the nearby River Estate is an old waterwheel.

The Santa Cruz Valley is being threatened by urban sprawl but there are still some very pleasant areas. Tucked away in the upper valley off La Sargasse Road is the farm of **Waterville** (tel. 676 7057). For those who wish to get to know the tropical fruits of Trinidad, one of Pam's tours of the property is highly worthwhile and costs US$ 6. A hike up to the head of the valley and down into Maracas Bay along an old mule track may also be arranged. At US$ 10, this includes return transport to the farm. Ensure you wear sensible footwear.

The north east and the road to Toco

The Eastern Main Road is the main route of escape out of Port of Spain and as such it tends to be busy. Unfortunately if you go touring you will find yourself on this road quite a lot.

Soon you will pass Mount Hope Hospital on the right. This is part of St Joseph, the first Spanish settlement. It was chosen in 1592 with the consent of the Amerindians, then later destroyed by Sir Walter Raleigh. Abercromby Street on the left leads to Maracas Royal Road and Maracas Valley. This turning is opposite the large, white Jinnah Mosque.

Maracas Valley is not to be confused with Maracas Bay which is on the other side of the Northern Range. Maracas Valley with its waterfall is a good place for hiking; a simple and well-signposted walk. The stream falls over 90 metres, however, it can be disappointing unless there have been heavy rains recently. There is a bed and breakfast here which makes a good base. A more ambitious hike is up to El Tucuche, the second highest peak at 957 metres, a day's walk, or you can even walk over to the north coast. Mount El Tucuche is a nature reserve, featuring some rare orchids and the Giand Bromeliad.

Back on the main road on the right is the **University of the West Indies,** which also has campuses on Jamaica and Barbados. On Trinidad are the faculties of agriculture, engineering, natural sciences and social sciences. Tours can be arranged by contacting the University.

Dominating the hillside to the north of here is the **Monastery of Mount St Benedict**. Construction was begun in 1912 by Dom Mayeulde Caigny and it was dedicated to 'Our Lady of Exile'. The structure is whitewashed with red tiles. It gives clear views of central Trinidad. Today the monastery also has a guesthouse, a drug rehabilitation unit, a pleasant tea shop, a basic restaurant and a shop selling a variety of religious items.

To reach the monastery turn up St John's Road. If you are on foot a bus shuttles people up and down the hill until around 1730. There are a number of interesting walks from the mount. There are two other interesting valleys running north. **The Caura Royal Road** follows the Tacariga River. Eventually you come to the Forestry Division Recreation Centre. This is good hiking country and there are several trails of differing lengths in the area.

Lopinot is a popular recreation park for Trinidadians. It has been well restored by the Tourism Development Authority. This land was once thought to be inhospitable jungle but it was developed by the

The manor house at the old Lopinot Plantation, which has been fully restored. It is now a popular recreational centre, complete with a small museum, picnic place and nature trails.

remarkable Charles Joseph, Compte de Lopinot, a refugee from the Haiti slave rebellion. He came to Trinidad with his family and 100 slaves, who he led up here to clear the land. The Compte must have been a man who inspired great loyalty or fear as his slaves never turned on him whilst he single-mindedly built up a plantation in this difficult terrain.

On the 478-acre site is the restored estate house which contains a few historical displays. Nearby is one of the cocoa drying stores, with a movable roof to shelter the beans from the rain. Further away are the great stone tombs of the Compte and his wife. There are several paths through the vegetation, and a modern picnic area.

Cleaver Woods on the outskirts of Arima is a small Amerindian museum. A large hut has been constructed from wood and there are exhibits of Amerindian implements. Entrance is free and the guides will give a quick talk about the place if asked.

Arima is the largest town in the area and acts like a communications hub. This was an old Carib settlement and many of its citizens claim to have Amerindian blood. Arima was made a Royal Borough in 1887. Every August the festival of Santa Rosa is held here. Nearby is Waller Field, the old American airbase.

Further east is the **Valencia Wildlife Sanctuary**, with 2,785 hectares (6,881 acres) of protected land which is home to 50 species of birds and a range of animals including deer, agouti, wild pigs, tatoo, and iguana. It has been a sanctuary since 1934 and is another example of Trinidad's commitment to conservation. The **Aripo Valley** nearby is also another naturalist's mecca.

From Valencia or Sangre Grande the road leads north east to Toco. This single road with few turnings off is ultimately a dead end but well worth the journey.

First you come to the wide Balandra Bay, then Cumana Bay and finally Gallera Point before turning on to the northern coast. All the bays along here are strikingly beautiful and many consider this the best part of the island though it takes more effort to get here.

Salybia Bay, **Toco**, and Matelot Bay will all be peaceful and picturesque. In some places cliffs drop dramatically into the sea. Parts of the coast are risky for swimming so ask the locals where to go. There are houses for rent in this area; check the local papers for details.

Toco itself is a sleepy place, where the route-taxis turn round. There is a police station, a rumshop, a couple of shops and a wonderful feeling of tranquility.

Western and central Trinidad

In Sangre Grande (pronounced Sandy Grandy), if you take the southern road instead of the northern road to Toco, you will soon reach the western coast at **Manzanilla**. The land here is split between two coconut estates. The beach is long, wide and excellent for swimming, with facilities provided by the Tourism Development Authority.

Further south is the **Nariva Swamp**; its 3,840 acres may be visited by boat. There are Red Howler monkeys, 58 other species of mammals, 171 species of birds, reptiles and fishes. Places of note include Bush Bush Island and Bois Neuf Forest.

Further south is **Mayaro Bay**. Along its length are a series of small villages. Again the beach is excellent. Guayaguayare is at the south west tip of Trinidad. Near here is Galeota Point, a centre of the oil industry. Offshore at night the lights of several oil rigs can easily be seen.

The Devil's Woodyard in southern Trinidad is the home of several mud volcanoes. Actually they are very placid and sit, slowly oozing mud..

The south west and southern coasts

The first major tourist sight south of Port of Spain is the **Caroni Swamp** and **Bird Sanctuary**. It is interesting for several reasons.

The Mangrove Forest is an area of mudflats which the mangroves sink their roots into. This produces a unique eco-system with oysters, mussels and crabs living below the waterline. It is also a breeding ground for many types of fish and home of the occasional alligator.

The boat tours for the Bird Sanctury leave at 1600. You are taken into the swamp and then as the light begins to fade thousands of Scarlet Ibis returning home for the night fill the sky as they settle into the tops of the mangrove trees. The Scarlet Ibis may steal the show but there are another 156 species of birds here as well.

There are two tour operators: David Ramsahai and Sons, (tel. 663 2207 or 645 4706) and Winston Nanan, (tel. 645 1305).

The Uriah Butler Highway continues south becoming the Solomon Hochoy Highway as it passes through the rich sugar-growing lands of central Trinidad. Off the highway there is the scenic village of **Claxton Bay** and the **Wild Fowl Trus**t at Point-a-Pirre.

This is a remarkable place. In 26 hectares of land within the petrochemical complex, endangered species of waterfowl and other birds are bred and reintroduced to the wild. These include the Scarlet Ibis, the Wild Muscovy duck, Amazon parrots and macaws. On site there is a car park and an Environmental Learning Centre which houses a small museum and library.

From San Fernando the roads branch off in several directions. The one to Princes Town takes you on to the **Devil's Woodyard**. Continue on towards New Grant then turn south at New Grant Primary School and drive for about three miles. If you do not have a car it is usually possible to find a taxi and negotiate a fare. Whatever the hype you hear about these mud volcanoes, it is a bit disappointing. There are from eight to twelve of them sitting in a field; each is about two metres high. The water buffalo in the neighbouring field are much more photogenic, but do not get too close, they dislike having their picture taken!

Other roads lead down to Erin or Moruga, small fishing villages on the south coast. The beaches along here are quite picturesque and safe for swimming.

Back in San Fernando the remaining road heads down to the south western point. At **La Brea** is the famous **Pitch Lake** where 38 hectares (95 acres) of asphalt lie beside the road. As you alight guides jump out offering tours; most are informative and can show you things you would otherwise miss, but bargain furiously before you accept their services.

Raleigh caulked his ships here in 1595 and realised the potential of the place, but commercial development did not begin until 1893. The asphalt has been exported to most of the world's continents. The Pitch Lake falls one metre every 12 years and nearby houses often sink with it a little. It began as a 25-metre high volcano but is now nine metres below sea level. It is still being excavated and sold.

It is possible to walk on most parts of the lake though one or two cracks and pools are liquid. One legend says that the gods buried an Amerindian village under the asphalt as a punishment for killing the sacred humming birds.

Further south is the industrial town of **Point Fortin**. There are a couple of bed and breakfasts here and some recreational facilities. Perhaps the town's biggest attraction is a sculptor's workshop tucked away down a street in one of the housing estates. The artist obviously does not want to advertise, yet his or her works are easy to see as they spill over into the garden.

Further west still is **Icacos**, a fishing village at the end of the headland. Nearby is an abandoned lighthouse which is slowly crumbling into the sea. Here Venezuela is much closer than Port of Spain.

Excursions

A number of companies offer guided tours of Trinidad, the main ones are listed below:

Great Caribbean Tours (Lady Young Road, Morvant, tel. 675 RENT). This group runs four trips: to the Asa Wright Nature Centre; to the sugar belt including a visit to one of the sugar refineries; to Maracas Bay on the north coast; and finally a city tour.

Hibiscus Tours Limited (Amral's Travel Head Office, 22 Tenth Avenue, Barataria, tel. 675 2537). This company offers the city and Maracas trips. In addition they go to Caroni Bird Sanctuary and down the south coast to include Point-a-Pierre, San Fernando and the Pitch Lake in one day. Other long trips include heading 'down the islands' on a boat tour, visiting Mount St Benedict then returning along the north coast road or going through the sugar belt to the Atlantic coast. Shorter itineries include a visit to a hibiscus nursery, which only takes an hour, or a six-hour tour to two plantation houses which includes lunch. A one day tour of Tobago is possible; this does not include the cost of a the flight but covers the transfer to a coach and a tour round Scarborough, Plymouth, Buccoo Reef and Pigeon Point.

Hospitality Services Ltd (61 Picton Street, Newtown, Port of Spain, tel. 628 6552). A number of standard tours is offered: one of the capital; another of Mount St Benedict's, San Fernando and Point-a-Pierre; a 'down the islands' tour including Maracas Bay and the Asa

Opposite, top: *The centre of the daytime social scene in Tobago is Store Bay, the closest beach to the Crown Point resorts. Changing rooms, snack bars and the boats heading out to the reef at Buccoo, all lie within a few metres of each other.*
Opposite, bottom: *Fort King George, above Scarborough, Tobago, is a fine example of the defences the British built to secure their colonial empire. Today it contains several old cannon, a powder magazine, a lighthouse, a tea room and the island's art gallery – something for all tastes.*

Wright Centre; one around the whole island; and a trip to the Caroni Bird Sanctuary. One particularly original tour laid on is to a panyard where you are shown the pans and given a chance to have a tinkle on them.

Sightseeing Tours (Galleria Shopping Centre, 12 Western Main Road, St James, Port of Spain, tel. 628 1051). Itineries include: Port of Spain, Maracas Bay, a whole island tour, the Asa Wright Centre, and the rainforest, 'down the islands', the Pitch Lake and Wild Fowl Trust, around the Savannah and Cleaver Woods coupled with Lopinot. Other less standard tours include an excursion to the Toco Bay area, or one of the historical buildings in and around the capital. A special flight is available which takes to the air in a Cessna 152 or 172 and covers almost the whole island.

Travel Trinidad and Tobago (69 Independence Square, Port of Spain, tel. 625 2201/5). Trips go out to Maracas Bay, 'down the islands', Port of Spain in the day or at night, the Asa Wright Centre, historic buildings around Port of Spain, or the Caroni Bird Sanctuary.

More unusual excursions are days out golfing, surfing or even kayaking across to Gasparee Island; the latter includes lunch on arrival there. Another water-borne expedition is aboard the *Jolly Roger*, a mock-up pirate ship. This sails out to five islets known as 'Los Cotarros' – the Parrots – from a Spanish legend of five daughters being turned into stone by their mother.

Twin Islands Tours (177 Tragarete Road, Port of Spain, tel. 622 5245). This group go around the capital or out to Maracas Beach, the Pitch Lake, the Wild Fowl Trust, Caroni Bird Sanctuary, the Asa Wright Centre, Maracas Bay, Toco, Lopinot, `down the islands' and one other place not mentioned above – the Devil's Woodyard.

Opposite, top: *The town of Plymouth, Tobago, is built on a point of land, which gives way on either side to fine stretches of beach. To the west is the famous Turtle Beach and, shown here, to the east, the picturesque Back Bay.*
Opposite, bottom: *The Argyle Waterfalls are now the most dramatic on Tobago, due to recent changes in the water supply. The route is clearly signposted off the Windward Road, just outside Roxborough. The pools are large enough to swim in.*

Trinidad is home to one of three naturally occurring pitch lakes in the world. Most of it is solid and with care it is possible to walk around on it. Here, a guide brings up some of the liquid bitumen from a crack in the surface.

Most of the tour organisers are flexible and will vary their itinery to meet the demands of their customers.

Other organisations which are worth consulting are:

The Forestry Division (Long Circular Road, Port of Spain, tel. 622 4521).

Trinidad and Tobago Field Naturalists Club (c/o Louisa Zuniaga, secretary, Errol Park Road, St Anns, Port of Spain, tel. 624 3321).

Annual events

January

New Year's Day a public holiday.

This is also a month of heated practising for calypsonians and steel bands. In the countdown to Carnival there are many concerts and much speculation about who is going to steal the show.

International Cricket Test matches take place at the Queen's Park Oval.

February

More concerts and then finally **Carnival** – four days of crazy celebration. The Carnival Saturday and Sunday (Dimanche Gras), parades are followed by Monday or 'Jour Ouvert'. Then comes the Tuesday; by Ash Wednesday everything is over till next year.

Occasionally Carnival may fall in March.

March

The Annual Flower Show.

Good Friday.

Phagwa, the Hindu festival celebrating the triumph of good over evil, the destruction of Molika by Lord Vishnu, the protector of the universe. The actual date varies and the event might be in April in some years.

The **Bath Tub Derby** is an oddball event that takes place on the Mayaro-Nariva River. It is hilarious to watch the contestants in fancy dress struggle to get their craft over the finishing line.

April

The **Cult of La Divina Pastora** is held at Siparia on the second Sunday after Easter. This is an Amerindian festival, worshipping the Virgin Mary.

May

The Islamic festival of **Eid ul Fitr** often falls in this month, though the date can vary considerably. It celebrates the end of Ramadan, the month of fasting. Prayer meetings are held and gifts exchanged.

The Hampton Games at the National Stadium.
Whit Monday public holiday.

June

Labour Day is a national holiday.

July

Hosay may fall in this month or soon after. It is a remembrance of the deaths of the Hussein and Hassan, grandsons of the Prophet Mohammed. It is now celebrated by most of the community and includes the excellent tassa drumming, which is Hindu in origin. Several nights of procession reach a climax when magnificently designed miniature mosques or Tadjahs are broken up to symbolise the funeral.

August

The beginning and end of the month are marked by **Emancipation Day** and then, **Independence Day**. This is a time of concerts, sports events and parades. Every year on Emancipation Day there is a powerboat race from Trinidad to Tobago.
Hindus observe **Krishna Leela** and **Ramleela**. They are respectively, re-enactments of the teachings of Lord Krishna and Ramleela.
The festival of **Santa Rosa** remembers the first of the New World saints. This involves a series of religious processions.

September

Republic Day, a national holiday is held on 24 September.

October

Divali is the premier event in the Hindu calendar, a time for celebration and joy. The triumph of good is sown with the lighting of Deyas, small pots containing candles. Families mark the occasion with feasts and presents.
The **Parang** festival, featuring local folk music and skills of excellence in different fields, is held.
San Fernando Arts Festival is held at the Naparima Bowl.
The **Steelband Festival** is held every two years. A large range of accomplished music is guaranteed. For the winning band it usually means lucrative contracts to play abroad.

November

The Best Village competition is a talent competition sponsored by the Prime Minister. At the show is a variety of dancing, singing and music.

December

Christmas in Trinidad has some features in common with the rest of the Christian world and some unique to this nation. It is a time for parang music and special cooking. Foods like black cake – made with fruits and alcohol – and pastellas, a meat filled pasty appear at this time of year.

Beaches

The popular beaches have had facilities provided by the Tourism Development Authority; these include toilets, showers and changing rooms. Some beaches have dangerous currents. In these cases the less well visited ones will have notices of warning; heed them. Other beaches will have trained lifeguards on them. A system of red flags is operated; do not swim between them as this signifies danger. The lifeguards are helpful so if you are unsure, ask. Do not leave your belongings unattended and if you come by car make sure it is locked.

Beaches have been covered in detail in the section on touring the countryside but here is a summary of their relative qualities:

Maracas Bay is very popular at weekends when there is a good beach scene, plenty of snack stalls and thousands of people out liming. There are some good waves for body surfing. It is quieter during the week.

Las Cuevas is the next bay east of Maracas. It is quieter but has excellent facilities.

Blanchisseuse along from Las Cuevas; even quieter.

Toco, Balandra Bays are remote and beautiful with no facilities.

Manzanilla on the Atlantic coast has good facilities. It is long and a quiet or busy stretch can be found according to preference. Probably the best Trinidad has to offer.

Mayaro, Erin and Moruga Bays offer long stretches of peace and quiet.

Vessigny Beach near La Brea has good facilities and is a popular place at weekends.

'**Down the islands**' have some nice inlets and small bays here and there. To really find seclusion take a boat out to Chacachacare.

Ballads above Maracas Bay. No-one escapes the jocular lines of this strolling bard, who can string a set of lyrics together as soon as he knows your name, much to the amusement of any onlookers.

Sports

Birdwatching

The prime locations are the Caroni Bird Sanctuary, Asa Wright Nature Centre, Nariva Swamp, Valencia and the Wild Fowl Trust. See the Touring the Countryside section for more details.

Cricket

Matches are held at the Queen's Park Oval, Port of Spain from January till June. The quality of the teams is excellent, needless to say. If you arrive out of season, matches are often held in recreation parks on Sundays.

Fishing

There are several places of repute around the coast, especially 'down the islands', where Franklin Delano Roosevelt came in the 1940s. If you need to hire a boat contact Mr Elton Pouchet of In Joy Tours, Cocorite, (tel. 622 8974). Fishing gear can be provided if enough warning is given. The current rate of hire to go out into the gulf is US$ 30 per hour.

For general information try the Trinidad and Tobago Gamefishing Association, Maraval Road, (tel. 622 3889). The secretary is Mr Sydney Johnson.

Golf

Of the four courses here two are in the north and two in the south. Each of these areas has a nine and an 18-hole course. All of them are accessible to visitors and fees are reasonable.

St Andrew's Golf Course, Moka, Maraval. This is the nearest course to Port of Spain, (yardage 3130 par 36, yardage 6085 par 72, USGAR 71.3). If you wish to play contact Mr Peter Hale or Mrs Verna Salandy on 629 2314. Caddies and a golf pro are available for hire at TT$ 20 and TT$ 25 respectively. The full 18 holes costs TT$ 70, nine holes are TT$ 45.

Chaguaramas Public Golf Course lies to the west of Port of Spain, (yardage 2814 par 33, yardage 5646 par 68, USGAR 66.5). The contact here is Mr McKenna on 634 4349 ext. 129. Clubs are available for TT$ 18 but there are no caddies or carts. The nine holes cost TT$ 35, but there are plans to upgrade the place to 18.

Pointe-a-Pierre Club is owned by the Trinidad and Tobago Oil Company Limited; ask for Mr Gomes on 658 1825. Caddies cost TT$ 20; clubs can also be obtained but not carts. Playing the 18 holes costs TT$ 60, (yardage 2645 par 34, yardage 5470 par 68).

Brighton Golf Course at La Brea is controlled by Lake Asphalt Limited. The nine holes are priced at TT$ 60. Mr Bill Ramrattan is the General Manager (tel. 648 7556).

Gyms attached to hotels

The Inn Gym, (Holiday Inn, Wrightson Road, Port of Spain, tel. 624 3502).

Valley Vue Gym, (Valley Vue Hotel, Ariapita Road, St Anns, Port of Spain, tel. 623 3511).

Gym

Body Works, (27 Philip Street, Port of Spain, tel. 625 3559, or West Mall, Westmoorings, tel. 637 4545).

Executive Health Club, (14 Gooding Village, San Fernando, tel. 657 5450).

Khell Fitness Club, (Gulf City Shopping Complex, La Romain, San Fernando).

Health Clubs

Trinis are a health-conscious people if the number of health spas is anything to go by. Some of the main clubs are included below, they are sub-divided into different categories.

Health Spas

Suddenly Slender Health Club, (Pembroke Street, Port of Spain, tel. 623 3503).
Suddenly Slender Health, (Bel Air Hotel, Piarco, tel. 664 4771/3 ext. 9)

Horse riding

The Bays and Grays Riding Centre run by Mrs Patricia Stollmeyer offer rides at an hourly rate of TT$ 50, (tel. 622 8752). They require 24 hours' notice but all equipment is provided. The stables are open from 1600 to 1800 on Mondays, Tuesdays, Wednesdays, Fridays and Saturdays.

Jogging

The Savannah in the centre of Port of Spain makes a natural jogging track; it is 2 1/2 miles in circumference. Every evening Trinis come out in their dozens to circle this huge park.

If you fancy something a little more adventurous, like charging through the bush and mud, up hill and down dale, then contact the Port of Spain Hash House Harriers, cross country runners with a difference. It's incredible to see the dedication with which they look for the trail that will take them back to where they started from. Once there the survivors celebrate their achievments with a 'down-down', Trini speak for a drink. A sense of fun is more important than any athletic prowess; go along if you enjoy meeting people. Contact Lorin Paton on 622 5806 or Peter Rees-Watkins on 628 2035/7, both during work hours. Runs take place every second Saturday.

Scuba

There is little diving off Trinidad. If this is a keen interest, Tobago has a lot more to offer and is geared up to the visitors' requirements.

Squash

Two courts have been recently constructed at the Valley View Hotel, (tel. 623 3511). The galleries can accommodate up to 100 spectators.

Surfing

The best places are at Maracas Bay and Las Cuevas, particularly over the winter. For more information contact the Surfing Association of Trinidad and Tobago's secretary Christopher De Freitas on 637 0763.

Tennis

There are lighted tennis courts at the Trinidad Hilton, (tel. 624 3211), and the Valley View Hotel, (tel. 623 3511).

Walking

Trinidad has a myriad of trails of differing complexity. If you require advice contact the Forestry Division, the Field Naturalist's Club or the various tour companies whose addresses are given in the Excursions section.

Watersports

These have not really been developed commercially. Tobago is more suited for this kind of activity.

Windsurfing

Windsurfers can be rented from Peter MacLean; call 623 4673 for details. For general information try the Windsurfing Association of Trinidad and Tobago's President, Phillip Archie, at 4A Archibald Street, Vistabella, (tel. 659 2457).

Other clubs of interest

For the addresses of the Forestry Division and the Field Naturalists Club see under Excursions. Other clubs that may be of interest include:

American Women's Club meets every second Tuesday. Call 622 6371 for details.

Canadian Women's Club of Trinidad meets every third Thursday, (tel. 623 7254).

Horticultural Society meets on the last Saturday of each month at 1500 hours. The mailing address is PO Box 252, Lady Chancellor Road, Port of Spain.

Rotary Club branches meet in different places at different times. Contact the Rotary Club, c/o Holiday Inn Hotel, (tel. 625 3361).

Soroptimist Club, has three branches. Call 663 1659 for more information.

UK Women's Club, meet at the Hilton Ballroom at 0930 every second Thursday of each month, (tel. 637 1320).

The Red House, seat of the Government of Trinidad and Tobago.

YMCA (tel. 625 9622 or 627 8764).
YWCA (tel. 627 6388).

Shopping and souvenirs

Duty free

The best places for this are the shops in the Departure Hall of Piarco International Airport or some of the boutiques in the Cruise Ship Complex. Outside this area some of the more select shops and department stores sell brand name watches, jewellery, perfumes, china, crystal, silverware and electrical goods. Savings of around 25% can be made depending on your country of origin.

Local products

The main shopping areas are Frederick Street in Port of Spain and High Street in San Fernando. A list of the better shopping malls follows:

Port of Spain and suburbs
De Market Place, Hotel Normandie, St Anns
Ellerslie Plaza, Saddle Road, Maraval
Long Circular Mall, Long Circular Road, St James
Royal Palm Plaza, Saddle Road, Maraval
Shoppes of Maraval, 3 Saddle Road, Maraval
Town Centre Mall, 16-18 Chacon Street
West Mall, Western Main Road, Westmoorings.

San Fernando
Cross Crossing Shopping Plaza, Cross Crossing
Gulf City Plaza, South Trunk Road
Plaza Montano, 40-42 High Street
Southland Shopping Mall, Cross Crossing Roundabout

For details on what to buy see the A to Z Information, section 11.

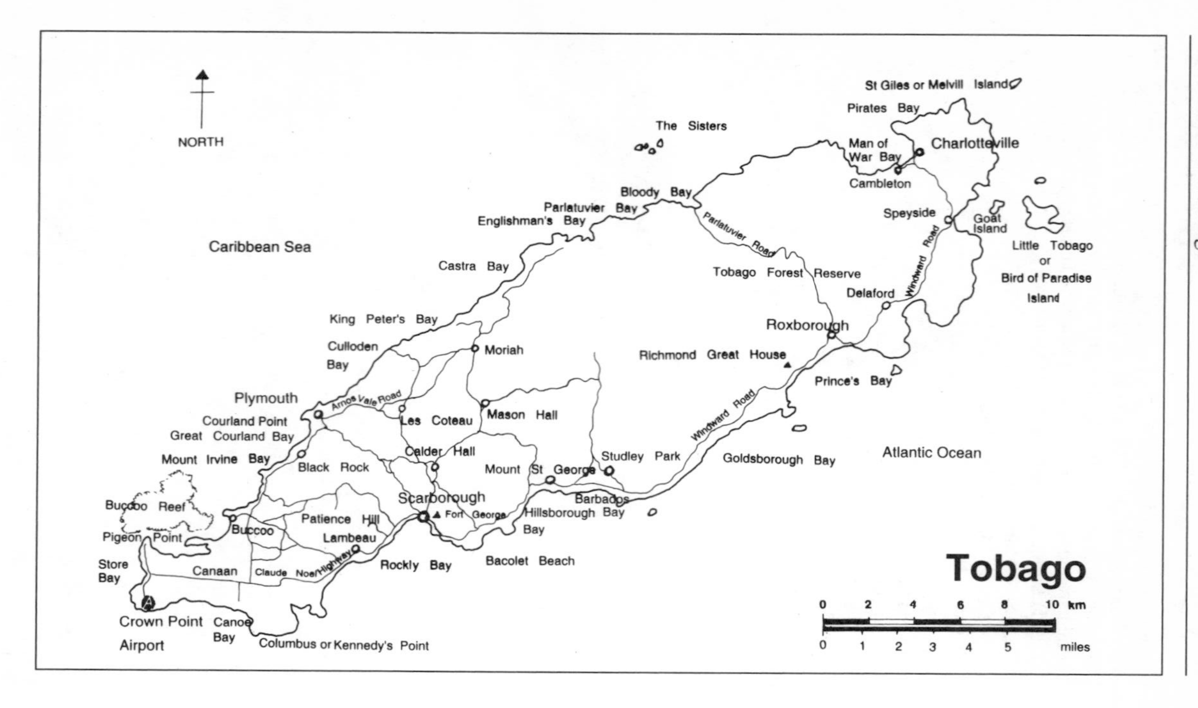
NORTH
St Giles or Melvill Island
Pirates Bay
The Sisters
Man of War Bay
Charlotteville
Cambleton
Bloody Bay
Parlatuvier Bay
Englishman's Bay
Speyside
Goat Island
Little Tobago or Bird of Paradise Island
Parlatuvier Road
Caribbean Sea
Castra Bay
Tobago Forest Reserve
Delaford
Windward Road
King Peter's Bay
Roxborough
Culloden Bay
Moriah
Richmond Great House
Prince's Bay
Plymouth
Arnos Vale Road
Les Coteau
Mason Hall
Courland Point
Great Courland Bay
Calder Hall
Studley Park
Goldsborough Bay
Atlantic Ocean
Mount Irvine Bay
Black Rock
Mount St George
Buccoo Reef
Scarborough
Fort George
Barbados Bay
Hillsborough Bay
Patience Hill
Pigeon Point
Buccoo
Lambeau
Store Bay
Canaan
Claude Noel Highway
Rockly Bay
Bacolet Beach
Tobago
0
2
4
6
8
10
km
Crown Point
Canoe Bay
0
1
2
3
4
5
miles
Airport
Columbus or Kennedy's Point

SIXTEEN

Tobago

Introduction

The classic tropical island, a place that has all the beauty expected of a Caribbean island yet the good news has not travelled too far. The high rise hotels have been kept away. They would like to be here, but Tobagonians will not let them. Instead you will find hamlets of gingerbread-style cottages, quiet country lanes, and long expanses of powdery sand.

It is a small world but the islanders like it that way. Many would throw their arms up in the air in horror at the thought of having to live in Port of Spain; all that noise, the crowds, and people passing without exchanging a greeting. Tobagonians say there is nowhere else they would rather be; now is your chance to see why.

When Defoe wrote the world famous *Robinson Crusoe* he talked about 'an uninhabited Island ... near the Mouth of the Great River of Oroonoque'; could this be Tobago? It is the kind of place you could imagine being shipwrecked on. While waiting for rescue, living on the fruits of the land and lying in the sun with the 'person Friday' of your choice.

Tobago is like Trinidad's little sister in many ways. They compliment each other so much, yet their relationship has at times been stormy. After being fought over so much between the powers of the day – no-one is quite sure how many times it changed hands – Tobago became a British possession. It became a typical slave colony till emancipation. After freedom it went through periods of prosperity and slump.

Tobago was in the grip of a severe recession when it came under the jurisdiction of the Trinidad authorities in 1888. This was resisted by the few dozen planter families who realised they would be losing their mini-kingdom; but ordinary people had already been travelling between the two islands for a number of years. Tobagonians have been angered by periods of neglect by some Trinidadian-based administrations but their House of Assembly has been preserved since union, and it has never been silent if it has felt that the island has been getting a poor deal.

The year 1986 saw the sweeping victory of the National Alliance of Reconstruction. The new Prime Minister was A.N.R. Robinson, a Tobagonian, who has ensured the island's voice has been heard. He retains enormous popularity here, even though the loud grumbles over the water about his policies, cost him the 1991 election. During the 1990 coup in Port of Spain not a thing stirred on Tobago; indeed the people were offended when they found themselves subject to the same curfew as Trinidadians.

The future is looking bright for the island. As well as foreigners many Trinidadians come for weekend breaks. The trick for Tobago is to enjoy the commercial success without losing its character, or getting any of the undesirable side-effects. So far so good.

Tobago's 50,000 people are almost all of African descent and it does not have the multi-culturalism of Trinidad. The population is almost uniformly Christian in belief so there is not the variety of festivals as on its sister island.

Scarborough is the capital; it resembles a small market town. A quiet place, it is the main administrative centre and terminal for the ferry. Crown Point out to the west is the main area of resorts.

A series of hills and ridges run down the centre of the island, reaching a height of 576 metres (1,890 feet). Tobago is 40 kilometres (21 miles), from Trinidad, 48 kilomtres (26 miles), long and 14 kilometres (9 miles) wide. The northern end of the island is rugged and less frequently visited.

The beaches of Tobago attract two types of visitor from across the oceans, the sun-seeker from the north and the Great Leatherback turtles. Local fishermen out trawling the bay with their huge seine nets mix pleasantly with both.

Arrival

By air

Crown Point Airport is under expansion; gone is its sleepy provincial feel. BWIA has now launched a series of direct flights to Europe which fly to London, Frankfurt and Stockholm once a week. There are six flights per day to Trinidad; five with BWIA and one with LIAT.

At the airport

The terminal is still small. There is a snack bar, bank and a tourist information desk outside the Customs and Immigration area. Crown Point has very much of an open-plan layout. There is a lay-by for taxis and plenty of car parking space.

Near the building is a bus stop for buses to Scarborough. A taxi to Scarborough will cost TT$ 40 against TT$ 0.75 on the bus. Public Transport Service Corporation bus tickets can be purchased at the left luggage department. The hotels in the Store Bay/Crown Point area are literally only a few hundred metres away from the airport. There are several car rental agencies in the near area as well.

By sea

Cruise ships

The cruise ship terminal in Scarborough is now open, with the harbour only recently dredged to allow ships to dock. With this facility available there is likely to be a significant increase in the number of liners visiting Tobago.

One thing passengers do not have to worry about is getting into town, you simply walk out the gates and you are there.

Yachting marinas

None exist at present, those arriving by sea may anchor in Scarborough's harbour. A quay is currently under construction at Plymouth. Alternately there are several safe anchorages around the coast.

Transport

Taxi

Most taxis have no meter but the drivers do run to fixed rates between destinations. Agree the fare before you set off. Taxis collect at Crown Point Airport and outside the larger hotels. The official ones have an 'H' registration, but Tobago also has several 'pirates' who operate in private 'P' registration cars. On the quiet routes the taxis have a monopoly.

Car rental

Visitors are urged to take advantage of any insurance schemes offered. The majority of roads are narrow and windy and bumps are

Seine fishing at Bloody Bay – a real community effort – everyone who helps gets a share of the catch. One end of the net is secured to a tree, the other is rowed out across the bay. After this all hands are needed to haul it in.

by no means uncommon. Virtually all the cars have an automatic gearbox. Here is a list of the leading companies:

Auto Rentals Ltd (North Side Road, Scarborough, tel. 639 0644) have a daily rental starting at TT$ 155 or TT$ 1,085 per week.
Baird's Rentals Ltd (Sangster's Hill Road, Scarborough, tel. 639 2528), provide small cars at the rate of TT$ 150 per day, or TT$ 900 per week. They also rent out ten-seater buses at TT$ 225 per day.
Crusoe Motors (Port Side, Scarborough, tel. 639 2174), can be contacted for details of rates.
Graham's Auto Rentals (Old Grange, Mount Irvine, tel. 639 0457), have Suzuki jeeps or air-conditioned cars; call for prices.
Peter Gremli Car Rental (Crown Point, tel. 639 8400), can hire out either jeeps at TT$ 140 per day or small cars for TT$ 160 per day.
Rattan RL Car Rental, (Shirvan Road, tel. 639 8271). The rates here begin at TT$ 125 daily, TT$ 800 weekly.

Rodriguez Travel (Clark Trace, Bethany, tel. 639 8507) start their prices at TT$ 150 per day, rising to TT$ 180. The weekly rate is from TT$ 1,050 to TT$ 1,260.
Singh's Auto Rentals (Grafton Beach Resort, Black Rock, tel. 639 0624), start their hire rates at TT$ 125 per day or TT$ 750 per month.
Spence Retails Service (Milford Road, Crown Point, tel. 639 8082), begin their rates at TT$ 160 daily and TT$ 1,120 weekly.
Sweet Jeeps, (Sandy Point, tel. 639 8553), have a small car rate of TT$ 150 per day; TT$ 125 for jeeps.
Tobago Travel (PO Box 163, tel. 639 8778), hire out their smaller cars for TT$ 165 daily, TT$ 1,155 weekly.
Toyota Rent-a-Car (Milford Road, tel. 639 7491), give their daily rate as TT$ 145 and their weekly, as TT$ 870.

Bicycle and moped rental

Bicycles can be hired in the Crown Point area by asking the guys hanging around the Store Bay beach facilities. They normally start at TT$ 40 per day but feel free to bargain.

There are two agencies offering scooters. Firstly **Blossom Scooter**, (tel. 639 8535), who are based at the Sandy Point Hotel and secondly **Modern Bike Rentals**, (tel. 639 3275). Make sure you get insurance and a crash helmet. VAT of 15% will probably be added to your bill.

Buses, maxi taxis and route taxis

Buses

Public transport on Tobago is not as comprehensive as on Trinidad but with care it is possible to get to most places. The Public Service Transport Corporation (PTSC), serves most routes with its regular blue buses but has recently introduced an Express Commuter Service (ECS). These buses will be white with red and black stripes. Operating between specially-designated stops these buses are air-conditioned but slightly more expensive.

Frequency of service varies depending on the population centres served. The Crown Point to Scarborough route runs every 30 minutes from 0500 till 2100. There is an hourly service between the Turtle Beach Hotel and the capital. Scarborough is linked to Roxborough four times per day, and another three buses pass through here to Charlotteville. Four trips are made from Roxborough to Bloody Bay. In addition it is hoped to use ECS buses for special excursions over weekends and holidays.

Some typical fares are listed below:

From	**To**	**Fare (TT$)**
Scarborough	Turtle Beach	0.75
Scarborough	Crown Point	0.75
Scarborough	Roxborough	1.00
Roxboroug	Charlotteville	1.00
Scarborough	Bloody Bay	2.25

There are some variations on routes: for example, it is possible to travel to Crown Point either via the Claude Noel Highway or Mount Pleasant.

Maxi taxis

There are not many on the roads. Those that are around tend to serve the Crown Point to Scarborough route along the Claude Noel Highway.

Route taxis

Sometimes these are difficult to figure out, as a number of 'P' registration cars are in this line of work. The best thing to do is to ask the driver, or to look out for their arm signals if you are standing beside the road. The route taxis are more numerous than maxi taxis, they tend to serve the Crown Point to Plymouth or Scarborough routes or go from Scarborough through Roxborough to Charlotteville. They are more pricey than the PTSC but still cheap. A sample fare is Plymouth to Charlotteville, at TT$ 3.

Accommodation

For hotel costs refer to foreword.

Crown Point area

High

Tropikist Beach Hotel (Crown Point, tel. 639 8512). A 33-room establishment of which eight are of a superior standard. The rooms come with air-conditioning, carpets, refrigerator, telephone and either a patio or balcony. The Tropikist has been in business since October 1977.

On-site amenities include a swimming pool with adjacent bar, restaurant serving three meals a day and a disco during the high season. Boating, scuba and car hire can be arranged from here. The hotel is on Milford Point, overlooking Store Bay. AMEX, MC, V.

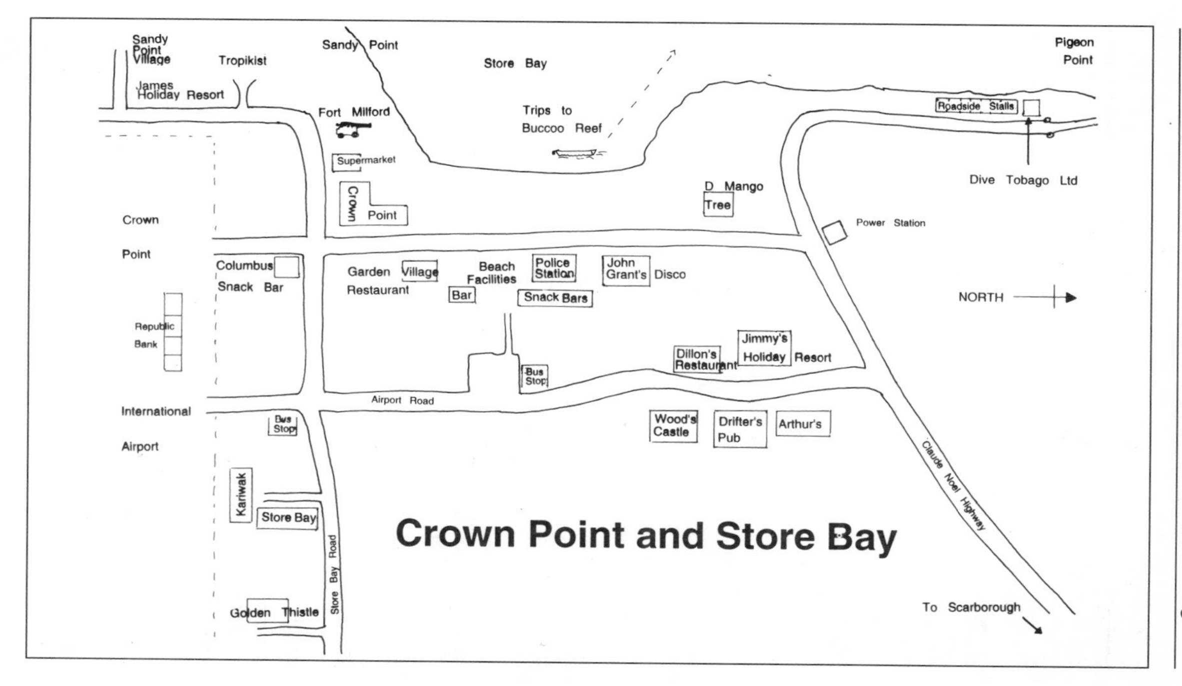
Sandy Point Village
James Holiday Resort
Tropikist
Sandy Point
Fort Milford
Store Bay
Trips to Buccoo Reef
Pigeon Point
Roadside Stalls
Dive Tobago Ltd
Supermarket
Crown Point
D Mango Tree
Power Station
Crown
Point
Columbus Snack Bar
Garden Village Restaurant
Beach Facilities
Bar
Police Station
Snack Bars
John Grant's Disco
NORTH
Republic Bank
Bus Stop
Dillon's Restaurant
Jimmy's Holiday Resort
International
Airport
Airport Road
Bus Stop
Wood's Castle
Drifter's Pub
Arthur's
Claude Noel Highway
Kariwak
Store Bay
Store Bay Road
Crown Point and Store Bay
Golden Thistle
To Scarborough

Middle

Kariwak Village (Crown Point, PO Box 27, Scarborough, tel. 639 8545). This hotel has won much praise primarily because of the hard work and dedication of the owners, Allan and Cynthia Clovis. A high priority is placed on training staff to the highest standards of service, which has led to a large number of repeat customers.

Accommodation is in nine originally designed cabanas, each constructed from local materials - raw teak, coral stone and bamboo. Each cabana is split into two bedrooms, each with air-conditioning and bathroom or shower.

Facilities include a swimming pool, bar and conference room. Live entertainment is laid on over the weekend in the well-regarded restaurant. The Kariwak has a complimentary transport service to Pigeon Point. AMEX, MC, V.

Crown Point Beach Hotel (Crown Point, PO Box 223, Scarborough, tel. 639 8781/3), is the largest hotel in the Crown Point area. It is beside the beach at Store Bay, with steps leading directly down to the sand.

The emphasis is on self-catering as all rooms have a kitchenette, though there is also a restaurant on site. There are studio apartments, larger apartments and cabanas available.

The hotel is spread over seven acres, with two tennis courts, a swimming pool and bar. Other facilities are table tennis, shuffleboard, TV room, and a grocery store. AMEX, MC,V.

Moderate

Arthur's Hotel (Crown Point, tel. 639 0196), is a 15-room hotel with restaurant and bar. It is only four minutes away from Store Bay. Rooms have air-conditioning and showers, with TV available.

Special vegetarian diets can be arranged here; the resturant is open for breakfast, lunch and dinner. Many things can be arranged through the front desk including bicycle, moped or car hire, tennis or sightseeing trips. AMEX, MC, V.

Golden Thistle (Store Bay Road, Crown Point, tel. 639 8521), has recently been enlarged to 26 rooms. Each comes with bath or shower, kitchenette, patio and colour TV. On site are a swimming pool, restaurant and bar. Some of the rooms are poolside; all are ideal for those looking for self-catering. MC, V.

Coral Reef Guesthouse (Milford Road, tel. 639 2536), is ten minutes' drive from the Crown Point area yet only five minutes' walk from the nearest beach. This is another place appealing to the self-catering market; each of the eight studios has its own kitchenette, though there is also a restaurant. Rooms come with TV and air-conditioning. MAP available; no credit cards.

Wood's Castle Holiday Resort (Crown Point, tel. 639 0803), a ten-room guesthouse next door to Drifter's Pub. Five minutes' walk from Store Bay. No credit cards.

Sandy Point Beach Club (Sandy Point, tel. 639 8533), is a 42-room condominium. Each room comes with air-conditioning, satellite TV and kitchenette. There is a small beach at the foot of the complex and hire car facilities on hand. AMEX, MC, V.

James Holiday Resort (Crown Point, tel. 639 8084), is a newly-built complex beside the Sandy Point Beach Club. The 14 rooms are air-conditioned with self-contained bathroom and kitchenette. Cars and jeeps are available for hire from the management. AMEX, MC, V.

Jimmy's Holiday Resort (Airport Road, Crown Point, tel. 639 8292), should not be confused with the above-mentioned resort. Jimmy's is on the road leading from the airport beside Dillon's Restaurant and opposite Arthur's on Sea.

There are 20 rooms here, each with air-conditioning and bathrooms. There is no swimming pool but it is only a short walk to the beach. AMEX, MC, V.

Budget

Store Bay Holiday Resort (Store Bay Local Road, Crown Point, tel. 639 8810), is a great place to stay for anyone looking for a self-catering holiday on a reasonable budget. Your host is Wilfred Best, who made his career in publishing before moving to the hotel business.

This resort is just off the Airport Road, a few minutes away from Store Bay. Each apartment comes with kitchenette and air-conditioning. There is a swimming pool, TV room, and sun deck on the premises, but no restaurant. Shops are situated nearby. AMEX, MC, V.

Samada Guesthouse (Milford Road, tel. 639 8312), six bedrooms and two self-catering apartments, each with two bedrooms. Each is air-conditioned with its own bathroom. All meals are available if requested and special honeymoon packages are available. Amex, MC, V.

In Plymouth, on the west coast, stands a monument to the Latvian settlers who came from the Baltic to the Caribbean in the seventeenth century. Beside this sculpture stands the village's diminutive post office, no larger than a garden shed.

Plymouth and the west coast

Top

Mount Irvine Bay Hotel and Golf Course (Mount Irvine, PO Box 222, tel. 639 8871/3), is one of only two hotels on Tobago that really caters to the sports enthusiast. In addition to the golf course reviewed in the Sports section, there are two tennis courts, a huge swimming pool, horse riding can be arranged and the beach is suitable for windsurfing.

Mount Irvine boasts two restaurants – the Beau Rivage and the Jacaranda – and five bars; one poolside, two in the hotel, one at the golf club and another down on the beach. There is a small arcade of shops and sound-proofed conference facilities.

In the hotel grounds are a selection of suites, premium or standard cottages and rooms. Each room contains two double beds, air-conditioning, bathroom and a patio or balcony. The hotel incorporates parts of an eighteenth-century sugar mill. Most of the rooms have been recently renovated.

A footpath leads down to the beach with its facilities. On most nights there are entertainments laid on for guests. AMEX, MC, V.

Grafton Beach Resort (Grafton, tel. 639 0191), is the only other hotel that caters to the sports enthusiast. On the five-acre site are two squash courts, a gymnasium, tennis courts, shuttleboard, a concessionary dive shop, windsurfing and a wide selection of water sports. The Mount Irvine Golf Course is nearby.

The resort has newly opened, the rooms being designed with comfort in mind. Each has a ceiling fan and air-conditioning, satellite TV, radio, mini-bar, bathroom and a balcony or patio. The two elegant suites come complete with jacuzzi. The Grafton is built upon Stone Haven Bay's fine beach, which is one of the Leatherback Turtle's main nesting sites. During the mating season the hotel organises watches.

The dining area overlooks the bar and entertainment area. Adjacent is the pool with its sunken bar. A shopping arcade, car hire desk and extensive car hire facilities are on site. The Grafton is highly recommended for those who seek an active holiday where the budget is not too much of a problem. AMEX, MC, V.

Turtle Beach Hotel (Plymouth, PO Box 201, tel. 639 2851/2), sits on one of the island's finest beaches. With 125 rooms, it is the largest resort on the island. Each room has a private bathroom, telephone, air-conditioning and balcony or patio.

Facilities include two tennis courts which can be lit for night play, a small swimming pool and complimentary watersports. There is a small conference centre, a restaurant and bars. Entertainments are laid on throughout the week on the premises. Rooms are available for handicapped guests. AMEX, MC, V.

Arnos Vale Hotel (Arnos Vale, PO Box 208, tel. 639 2881/2), is set in 400 acres of private grounds. The resort is centred around a nineteenth-century estate house which now houses the reception area, bar and dining room. Guest accommodation is in 30 rooms located in cottages in the gardens or in a block on the bay where the swimming pool and beach-side bar are located. The Italian management can organise a range of activities including tennis, archery, canoeing, golf (off site), hiking along the pleasant clifftop walk or birdwatching. AMEX, MC, V.

Moderate

Cocrico Inn (Plymouth, PO Box 287, tel. 639 2961), is a small, friendly guesthouse on a peaceful side-street in Plymouth. Its the kind of place you come to for peace and quiet rather than the hectic nightlife. A hide out for Latvians on a pilgrimage, naturalists or watercolour artists. There are two beaches within easy reach; it just depends on whether you turn left or right as you leave.

On site there are 16 rooms; singles, doubles or triples. There is a bar/restaurant area, TV room and swimming pool. Kitchenettes, MAP or AP is available if supplements are paid. AMEX, MC, V.

Old Grange Inn (Mount Irvine, PO Box 297 Buccoo, tel. 639 0275). A small guesthouse adjoining the Papillon Restaurant. The 18 rooms come with air-conditioning and private bathroom. Amenities include a TV room, and a swimming pool is being planned. The Grange Beach is a two-minute walk away. AMEX, MC, V.

Lawrenceville Guesthouse (Plymouth Road, tel. 639 4167), is on the Plymouth Road, five minutes' drive from either Scarborough or Turtle Beach. It is situated in a quiet residential area and has eight rooms, some doubles, some singles. Four have self-catering facilities; all have a bathroom or shower. No credit cards.

Scarborough area, the east and north coasts

High to top

Blue Waters Inn (Batteaux Bay, Speyside, tel. 660 4341), is located near the island's best birdwatching and diving sites. It is the base for Dive Tobago and a stopping point for glass-bottomed boat tours. Amenities include tennis courts and windsurfing. The bay is particularly striking.

Accommodation can be in self-catering units that sleep four people or bedrooms with private showers or toilets. There are a variety of dining plans from room only to all meals being provided. The restaurant has a fixed menu. The bar is on the waterfront; dress is always informal. AMEX, MC, V.

High

Palm Tree Village (Little Rockley Village, Milford Road, tel. 639 4347), is to the west of Scarborough with a bay almost all to itself. It is a collection of two or four-bedroom villas. Each is air-conditioned, with kitchenette, telephone, TV, and a patio. Most activities can be arranged from the front desk. AMEX, MC, V.

Richmond Great House, near Roxborough, is one of Tobago's best preserved plantation buildings. In addition to being a guesthouse it also contains the country's best collection of African sculptures.

Medium to high

Man-O'-War Bay Cottages (Charlotteville Estate, tel. 660 4327), is located on a cocoa plantation. There are six cottages each with one to four bedrooms. All have been renovated and fitted with kitchens and beach-side patios. This is a prime location for snorkelling, birdwatching, fishing or hiking. AMEX, MC, V.

Medium

Richmond Great House (Belle Garden, tel. 660 4467), dates back to the late 1700s. This former plantation house stands on the crest of a hill which affords it sweeping views of the surrounding countryside. Set in its own gardens, it has its own pool and bar. There are six units here, one with two bedrooms.

Rates include breakfast and may be extended to include dinner as well. The cooking is a well-regarded selection of local dishes. There is a complimentary transport service, picking up and returning guests to the airport.

What the house is truly remarkable for is the finest collection of Africana in this country. The owner, Professor Hollis Lynch, is usually absent as he now lectures at Columbia University. He has amassed an intriguing display of sculptures, masks and tapestries which now adorn the rooms and corridors. Non guests are welcome in the dining room, but prior reservation is preferred. BB standard, MAP available. No credit cards.

Moderate

Della Mira Guesthouse (Bacolet Street, PO Box 203, Scarborough, tel. 639 2531), is on the outskirts of the capital, overlooking the bay. Your hosts are Neville and Angela Miranda, who have had many years' experience in the Tobago hospitality scene. Bacolet Beach is a few minutes' walk away and there is a swimming pool on site.

It is a small place with 14 air-conditioned rooms. Each has a balcony and its own bathroom. On site is a restaurant serving local dishes, a beauty salon, and a bar/disco, La Tropicale. AMEX, MC, V.

Bougainvillaea Beach Towers, (Studley Park, tel. 639 4622), overlooks Barbados Bay. There are eight bedrooms either in a separate house or apartments. On the property are a swimming pool, badminton court, table tennis, restaurant and bar. No credit cards.

Budget

Jacob's Guest House (Carrington Street, tel. 639 2271), is right in the centre of Scarborough. There are ten rooms and three apartments here, all at very reasonable prices. No credit cards.

Almandez Beach House (Charlotteville, PO Box 151, Scarborough, tel. 639 2631), has a three-bedroom apartment on the beach. The accommodation has electric fans, bathroom, TV and a large kitchen. No credit cards.

The Bed and Breakfast Association of Tobago

With over a dozen bed and breakfast homes on Tobago the Association is flourishing. Each member has a reputation for friendliness and good service. The Association is highly recommended, if living with a family appeals to you.

Most rates fall into the US$ 20 to US$ 25 range but it is worth checking first as some houses may cease taking in guests, others fall outside this price range, and may be considered too expensive for those on a budget. Credit cards are not accepted. A list of the current hosts follows:

Ann's Villa (Bacolet Street, Scarborough, tel. 639 5200), is opposite Bacolet Beach. There are two rooms available with a shared

bathroom. Self-catering is available and there is a small shop on the premises.
Federal Villa (Scarborough, tel. 639 3926), is near the botanical gardens. Guests can be picked up from the airport.
Hampden House (Hampden, Lowlands, tel. 639 7313), has three bedrooms with ceiling fans. It is five minutes' drive from the beach.
Harris House (Bacolet, near Scarborough, tel. 639 2111), is near Bacolet Beach. The rooms are air-conditioned.
Hillcrest (Bethany, tel. 639 4122), has air-conditioned rooms.
Midway Point (Mason Hall, tel. 639 6581), has basic amenities but is the cheapest place on the island at US$ 12 per night. It is inland from Scarborough.
Peterson's Villa (Government House Road, tel. 639 2939), is on the outskirts of Scarborough.
Pentridge Lodge (Plymouth, tel. 639 4129), offers assistance in travelling to and from the airport but is double the price of most other bed and breakfasts.
Points Inn (Buccoo, tel. 639 7064), has pleasantly furnished rooms available.
Sea Edge (Mount Irvine, tel. 639 9052), overlooks the golf course.
Sotto Vento (Gleneagles Drive, Mount Irvine, tel. 639 2976), is more expensive than most bed and breakfasts but near the beach.
Tony's House (Carnbee, tel. 639 8836), is the home of Mr Lloyd Anthony, the secretary of the Tobago branch. He is a friendly and helpful host who is willing to pick up guests from the airport. The house is set in attractive surroundings and the rooms air-conditioned.
Windy Hill (Bethel, tel. 639 8338), has two rooms suitable for double occupancy.

Villa rental

For villa rental try contacting one of the following addresses:

Biscot Villa (PO Box 185, Scarborough, tel. 639 8855).
Summer Hill Villa (Arnos Vale, tel. 625 8945).
Tobago Villas Agency (PO Box 30, Scarborough, tel. 639 8737).

Places to eat

Dining out

Reservations are recommended for most places and essential for some. Casual or casually smart dress is acceptable everywhere;

swimwear is not. Information on dining places is available from the Division of Tourism. There are no fast food outlets on Tobago.

French

Le Beau Rivage (Mount Irvine Golf Course, tel. 639 8871). An open-air restaurant overlooking the fairways. It is open seven days per week from 0630 till 2300. The dinner menu is excellent with a wide range of mainly seafood dishes to choose from. Try the lobster with ginger and spring onions or the rum lobster thermidor. Casually smart dress is suggested. A meal here will cost TT$ 150 and upwards. AMEX, MC, V.

Seafood dishes

Jemma's Seafood Kitchen (Speyside, tel. 660 4066). There are tables inside but the best place is on the raised porch overlooking the sea. By evening there is a cooling breeze blowing in from the Atlantic. The service is pleasant and the dishes all local.

Jemma's is normally open for lunch but if you wish to have dinner it is necessary to book in advance. Dinner consists of a three-course meal for the fixed price of TT$ 40; alcoholic drinks are not served. No credit cards.

Blue Crab, (Robinson Street, Scarborough, tel. 639 2737). A popular lunchtime dining place, which specialises in local recipes. Dinner is served throughout the high season and on Wednesdays and Fridays in the low season. The tables are on the large verandah.

Your host is the effusive Alison Sardinha, a cookery expert who loves her work. The service is prompt and the food well prepared. Meals are served with a good selection of local vegetables. If you wish to eat lobster order it the day before. A meal will cost between TT$ 30 and TT$ 50. AMEX, V.

Papillon (Old Grange Inn, Buccoo Junction, tel. 639 0275). The speciality here is seafood. Dining is in the air-conditioned bar/ restaurant. Try the Papillon seafood platter. Vegetarian and meat dishes are available. Open all week round for lunch and dinner. Three courses here will cost from TT$ 60 to TT$ 120. AMEX, MC, V.

Dillon's Seafood Restaurant (Airport Road, Crown Point, tel. 639 8765). Opposite Drifter's Pub, Dillon's is open from 1800 every day except Mondays. Dinner ranges from TT$ 60 to TT$ 100. No credit cards.

Chinese

Jatt's Harbour Wok (Milford Road, tel. 639 2745). After recent renovation Jatt's has changed from being mainly a takeaway to a 28-seat restaurant. It is open from 1000 to 2300 on each day except Sunday. Meals here cost between TT$ 20 and TT$ 40. No credit cards.

Continental and local

Old Donkey Cart (Bacolet Street, Scarborough, tel. 639 3551). A wine bistro set in an attractive white and green colonial house. The owner, Gloria Jones, has succeeded in bringing a new type of eating establishment to the island. Dining, accompanied by classical music, is either outside on the terrace or beside the wine racks. The music and subdued lighting creates an intimate ambiance.

The a la carte menu has a wide range of fish and meat dishes with a continental or local flavour. There are also one or two vegetarian dishes. Other notable features are the European cheeses and the large selection of German wines. Recommended dishes include the Tobagonian mixed salad, homemade pasta or if you fancy something a little spicier, the Calcutta shrimp.

The Old Donkey Cart is open from 1200 till 0200 during the week, except on Wednesday when it is closed. Over the weekends the hours are from 1830 till 0200. Arrangements can be made to return people to their hotels. Prices for a meal range from TT$ 50 to TT$ 150. AMEX, MC, V.

The Sugar Mill and **Jacaranda** (Mount Irvine Bay Hotel, Mount Irvine, tel. 639 8871/8800). Two high quality restaurants serving a good selection of meat and seafood dishes; some traditional favourites, others new and interesting, such as braised chicken in a peanut sauce. Entertainments are laid on most nights. Meals start at TT$ 50. AMEX, MC, V.

Kiskadee (Turtle Beach Hotel, Plymouth, tel. 639 2851/2). The a la carte menu has a good selection of local and international dishes. Entertainments are laid on most nights. AMEX, MC, V.

Italian

La Tartaruga (Idlewild, Scarborough, tel. 639 1861). Located off Wilson Road on a hill overlooking the capital, this is a new venture opened by Gabriele de Gaetano and Andria Xavier. Dining is in a spacious home accompanied by light Italian music.

There is no a la carte menu but a set meal of a minimum of five courses, which is explained in great detail by your hosts. Italian wines and liqueurs are available to accompany the excellent cuisine. La Tartaruga is closed on Tuesdays; on other days the first sitting is at

1930. Reservations must be made in advance; special diets can be catered for. The set meal will vary at around TT$ 110 to TT$ 170. No credit cards.

Arnos Vale Hotel (Arnos Vale, tel. 639 2881/2). An Italian dish is always laid on though much of the menu consists of Caribbean dishes. The menu for each day varies. Dining is in the converted plantation house with fine views of the bay. Reservations are advised for non residents. Prices begin at TT$ 50. AMEX, MC, V.

Mexican

Howling Cayote (Black Rock, tel. 639 8694). Probably the country's oddest-sounding restaurant, this is a one-woman operation run by Joleen Decle. It is a small wooden house with veranda. Each day a local and a Mexican dish are available, yet the place is sufficiently small that if a group rings ahead they can choose the dishes prior to arrival.

Lunches are prepared on Tuesdays; dinners are in one sitting at 1900 on all days except Tuesday and Thursday. Meals cost around TT$ 20 to TT$ 50. No credit cards.

Local cooking

Kariwak Village (Crown Point, tel. 639 8442). This hotel has built up a reputation for good Caribbean food; its buffet is especially recommended. Meals over the weekend come with live entertainment. A meal will cost from TT$ 40 to TT$ 120. AMEX, MC, V.

Rouselle's (Bacolet Road, tel. 639 4738). Each night a small choice of local dishes is on the menu with the emphasis being on freshness. The pies and ice cream are all home made, as is the Rouselle's punch, which is made like a daquiri. Special diets can be catered for.

The building is nearly 100 years old and was previously a dance hall. Now the decor is potted plants in a white room, cooled by ceiling fans. Closed on Sundays and open for lunch only on Fridays; during the rest of the week all meals are served. The price at TT$ 70 to TT$ 120, includes all three courses. AMEX, MC, V.

Cocrico Inn (Plymouth, tel. 639 2961) offers a selection of local dishes on its menu. Dinner choices include lobster, stewed or curried chicken and flying fish. A vegetarian dish is available. Breakfast, lunch and dinner are served here; the latter will cost at least TT$ 60. AMEX, MC, V.

Steak Hut (Sandy Point Beach Club, Sandy Point, tel. 639 8533/4). On Wednesdays there is a curry dinner available for TT$ 50. Fridays sees live entertainment and for TT$ 65, a three-course meal and all the rum punch you can drink. Do not forget the surcharges on top of this; 10% service and 15% VAT. AMEX, MC, V.

Golden Spoon (Crown Point, tel. 639 8078). This is open throughout the week from 0800 to 2300. On some nights there is live entertainment as well. A meal here will be between TT$ 25 and TT$ 100. No credit cards.

Drift Wood (Blue Waters Inn, Speyside, tel. 660 4341). Open for breakfast, lunch and dinner, it serves a mixed menu with a choice of two dishes for dinner. AMEX, MC, V.

D Mango Tree (Store Bay) serves a selection of local and Chinese dishes. No credit cards.

Village Restaurant (Store Bay, tel. 639 8442) is beside the beach area. No credit cards.

Black Rock Cafe (Black Rock). No credit cards.

Whitelily Diner (Plymouth). No credit cards.

Cafe eating

Fort King George After the long climb to look around the fort it is now possible to get a hot or cold drink, snack or pasty before the walk back. Open during the daytime. No credit cards.

Teaside (Lambeau, tel. 639 4306). Enjoy one of 26 types of tea under the thatched roof. Coffee, fresh juices, cakes, biscuits and pizza are also on the menu. The opening hours are from 1000 to 1800 on Monday through to Thursday and Saturday, 1000 till 2000 on Friday and 1500 to 1800 on Sunday. Stopping here could cost between TT$ 5 to TT$ 45. No credit cards.

Snack bars

Buddy's Food Delight (Scarborough, tel. 639 3355). Open from 0700 to 2300 on Monday through to Saturday. A variety of local foods is available. Buddy's is in the centre of Scarborough Mall. A filling meal here will cost between TT$ 10 to TT$ 50. No credit cards.

Miss Esmee's and **Miss Jean's** opposite Store Bay and beside the beach facilities are very popular eating places. Crab and dumplings, chicken and pilau are amongst the wide range of dishes available. The price will be around TT$ 10 to TT$ 20. No credit cards.

Columbus Snack Bar (Crown Point), sells rotis and chicken and chips. No plush fittings here, just cheap, filling food. A meal here will cost between TT$ 8 and TT$ 20. No credit cards.

Chez D's (Garden Side Street, tel. 639 2089). A centrally-located bakery selling a range of cakes, pies and pastries. No credit cards.

The streets of Scarborough abound with neat houses, surrounded by well-kept flower beds. Many Tobagonians are keen gardeners, raising a profusion of scarlet poinsettias and chaconia.

Basics

Banks

The commission rate is the same in Tobago as in Trinidad. Banks can be found in Crown Point, Scarborough and Roxborough. Some may have restricted opening hours. If you find yourself short of cash try the hotels; but check the rate you are being offered before you change.

Here is a selection of the main banks:
Bank of Commerce (tel. 639 2811)
Bank of Nova Scotia (tel. 639 2761)
National Commercial Bank (tel. 639 3111)
Republic Bank (tel. 639 2561)
Royal Bank (tel. 639 2404)
Worker's Bank (tel. 639 2459).

Communications

The phone system is identical to Trinidad's. It is operated by Telecommunications Services of Trinidad and Tobago. Most hotels will allow guests to make international calls. If this is not possible there is a Textel office in Scarborough.

The post service is a mixture of addresses and PO boxes. The Main Post Office (tel. 639 2414), is in Scarborough, just off Wilson Road on (surprise, surprise) Post Office Street.

Emergency services

Dial 990 for the police in emergencies. For other routine calls contact the nearest police station. The police are issued with black and grey uniforms and many wear old-fashioned style pith helmets. Some police stations are listed:

Scarborough (tel. 639 2512)
Roxborough (tel. 660 4333)
Charlotteville (tel. 660 4388).
Call 990 for an ambulance or the fire brigade.

Library

Between the new shopping centre and the bus station in Scarborough stands the library. It is quite a large and impressive building, open during office hours.

Medical

Scarborough Hospital is along Fort Street just before you get to the top of the hill and the actual fort. It is equipped to deal with accidents and emergencies across the whole island. The telephone contact number is 639 2551.

There are three island pharmacies:
Dependable Drugs, Roxborough
Milford Drugs, Milford Court, Bon Accord (tel. 639 9407)
Tsoi's Pharmacy, NIB Mall, Scarborough (tel. 639 3383).

Dial 990 for an ambulance, or call the Scarborough Hospital.

Newspapers

Tobago has the same papers as Trinidad; it also has one indigenous publication, the *Tobago News*, which appears every Friday. The Trini press are the *Trinidad Guardian* and the *Trinidad and Tobago Express*. Weekly and weekend journals are for sale but foreign papers are difficult to obtain.

Places of worship

The island is almost uniformally Christian; there are a large number of denominations on Trinidad but less here.

Denomination	Church, address and telephone number	Time of main service
Anglican	St Andrews, Scarborough (tel. 639 2485).	Sunday 0730
Methodist	Methodist Church, Fort Street, Scarborough.	Sunday
Roman Catholic	St Joseph, Bacolet Street, Scarborough.	Sunday

Tourist information

On Tobago this is the responsibility of the Division of Tourism, which is responsible to the Tobago House of Assembly, a sign of the island's autonomy. Nevertheless it does work closely with the Tourism Development Authority of Trinidad.

The main office is located on the top floor in the new shopping mall in Scarborough town centre, (tel. 639 2125). The staff are helpful and efficient. The other branch is at Crown Point Airport, (tel. 664 5196).

A range of free maps is available in these offices and in many of the hotels.

Nightlife

Cinema

There is one cinema in Scarborough on Carrington Street. The usual programme is a double bill, which will cost from TT$ 7 to TT$ 10 depending on the seat.

Theatre

The **Buccoo Folk Theatre** puts on an entertaining mix of dancing and calypso on Thursdays at the Turtle Beach Hotel, (tel. 639 2851/2).

Discos

Sunday School, no seriously, that's what it's called, and you certainly do not have to be a devout believer to be a member of this flock! This event has become a Tobagonian institution. From about 2200 every Sunday the seafront at Buccoo village becomes the centre of a huge party. There is a bar selling drinks and a DJ playing soca and dub reggae. Huge numbers of people turn up each week to lime, dance and 'wine'. A long line of cars snake back down the road.

Eco-tourism in Trinidad and Tobago?

Being 'green' is something every organisation would like to claim, it makes them sound more caring and helps to sell their products. The new buzzword in the travel business is 'eco-tourism'. This is tourism which works hand in hand with the local community and ensures that the host nation can absorb the visitors without too many of the negative side-effects such as pollution, debasing of culture, increasing crime, AIDS, drugs etc.

One country that has made a name for itself in this kind of work is Belize. The Trinidad and Tobago Tourism Development Authority wants to encourage development in a similar way. Legislation has been brought in to encourage this, however, there has been damage to the local environment. Parts of the Buccoo Reef have been damaged by boats or people walking on the coral.

With such a variety of flora and fauna these islands have already made a name for themselves amongst naturalists. The government has had a long tradition of preserving large areas of land and creating nature reserves. The Caroni Bird Sanctuary and Little Tobago are good examples; though not all visitors are interested in this type of holiday.

Part of being environmentally sensitive therefore means ensuring that the development is carried out at a sensible rate. The sea and beaches must not become polluted or it will be a case of killing the goose that lays the golden egg.

Some of the legislation which has been enacted helps in this field. Only low-rise hotels are allowed on Tobago at present and projects have to meet certain environmental standards. Yet there is considerable pressure from big business to allow large-scale exploitation of the island which must be resisted if the country is to remain a green and pleasant land.

If you like partying do not miss this. It can go on to any time up to 0600; some hardy people go straight on to work from here. The taxis all know where the Sunday School is so you should have no problem getting back to your hotel.

John Grant Disco (tel. 639 8793), is a single-storey building down on Store Bay. It has DJ music from 2100 till early in the morning every day except Sunday. The music is a mixture of soca and reggae; there is a cover charge.

Club Christie (Level 3, Youngs Building, Piggott Street, Scarborough). This is the island's newest nightspot, it has become quite popular. Open on Fridays and Saturdays, the cover charge is TT$ 10 and free for women on Fridays, the busiest night.

La Tropicale (Della Mira Guesthouse, Bacolet Street, Scarborough, tel. 639 2531) is a bar and disco on the waterfront. Admission free; the music is soca, calypso and reggae.

Bars

Starting Gate Pub (Shirvan Road, tel. 639 4283). This is designed on the lines of a British bar, complete with darts. It is built on the site of the old race track and the starting gate still lies in the back garden, hence the name of the pub. On Thursdays, Fridays and Saturdays it stays open late, has a DJ and charges admission.

The charge varies from TT$ 10 to TT$ 20 depending on the night; some of this is given back in drinks vouchers. Friday is 'ladies night'. The Starting Gate is one of the most frequented drinking places and is on the main road between Buccoo and Crown Point.

Drifters Pub in the Crown Point area, just down from Arthur's on Sea. A small bar with partitioned bays; sometimes it's quiet, sometimes it's so busy even the air-conditioning cannot cope.

Cabin Pub, Carrington, Scarborough; a lively rum shop near the harbour.

Hotel entertainment

As Tobago is relatively quiet a number of hotels put on their own 'in house' entertainments; these often take place in the restaurant areas. Non guests are welcome at these functions.

Crown Point Beach Hotel (Crown Point, tel. 639 8781/3), puts on the following events: on Sundays a folk group, Wednesday is steel band night, and Fridays and Saturdays feature live bands. The entertainments are timed to last from 2000 till 2200.

Grafton Beach Resort (Black Rock, tel. 639 9444), has steel bands appearing on Sundays, Fridays and Wednesdays, a live band on Monday and Thursday, Calypso and limbo on Tuesday and a folk group on Saturday. There is entertainment on each day of the week followed by a disco till the early hours.

Kariwak Village (Crown Point, tel. 639 8442), has live bands on Fridays and Saturdays from 2000 till 2300. This accompanies the excellent buffet laid on for these nights.

Mount Irvine Bay Hotel (Mount Irvine, tel. 639 8871), puts on events every night except Wednesdays. On Mondays there is a slide show on Tobago, a rum punch party accompanied by a steelband on Tuesdays, Thursdays and Sundays feature live bands, Friday is the folk group evening, whilst on Saturday a pianist plays.

Palm Tree Village (Little Rockley Bay, Lambeau, tel. 639 4347), has live entertainment from Thursday to Saturday all year till 2200, and over the whole week during the peak holiday period.

Sandy Point Beach Club (Sandy Point, tel. 639 8533) lays on a calypso band for Wednesday evenings and a steel band for Fridays.
Turtle Beach Hotel (Plymouth, tel. 639 2851/2), puts entertainments on all week. Saturday through to Monday nights have a steel band; on Thursday the folk group mentioned in the Theatre section above, perform. On the other nights a live band play.

The sights of Tobago

The Crown Point Area

The International Airport is tucked into the western tip of Tobago; around it is the main area of hotel development with several bars and restaurants.
Store Bay, a popular beach just down from most of the hotels, was originally named Stoer after one of the early Dutch colonists. Opposite are the beach facilities and a number of snack bars including Miss Jean's and Miss Esmee's, both famous for their curried crab and other local dishes. There is a bar and covered seating across from the bay, this is the centre of the beach scene on the island.
Buccoo Reef is undoubtedly the country's most famous coralline formation. It is the result of over 10,000 years of growth; when pieces are broken off hundreds of years of nature's work may be destroyed. Up to 39 different types of the hermatypic, or reef-building, corals may exist here. The reef can be seen by divers or by glass bottom boats and snorkelling.

There are two operators recommended by the Tourism Development Authority:
Hew's Tours, Buccoo, Coral Gardens, Tobago, (tel. 639 9058).
Tobago Reef Tour Association, Buccoo Point, Tobago, (tel. 639 8519).

Alternatively, just take a walk down to Store Bay, where tour boats depart from regularly. The TT$ 30 trip includes a leisurely cruise, snorkelling gear and some rum punch. It takes about 20 minutes to reach the reef.

The **Nylon Pool** lies half way out on the way to Buccoo Reef. This is an area of shallow water above a sandbank where it is possible to get out and walk around. Some areas of reef have been badly damaged in the past; please ensure you take care not to add to this.
Fort Milford guards Store and Milford Bays. It was built by the British in 1777. In 1781 the French landed and captured it; 12 years later the British got it back. It is a low stone building, set in a garden

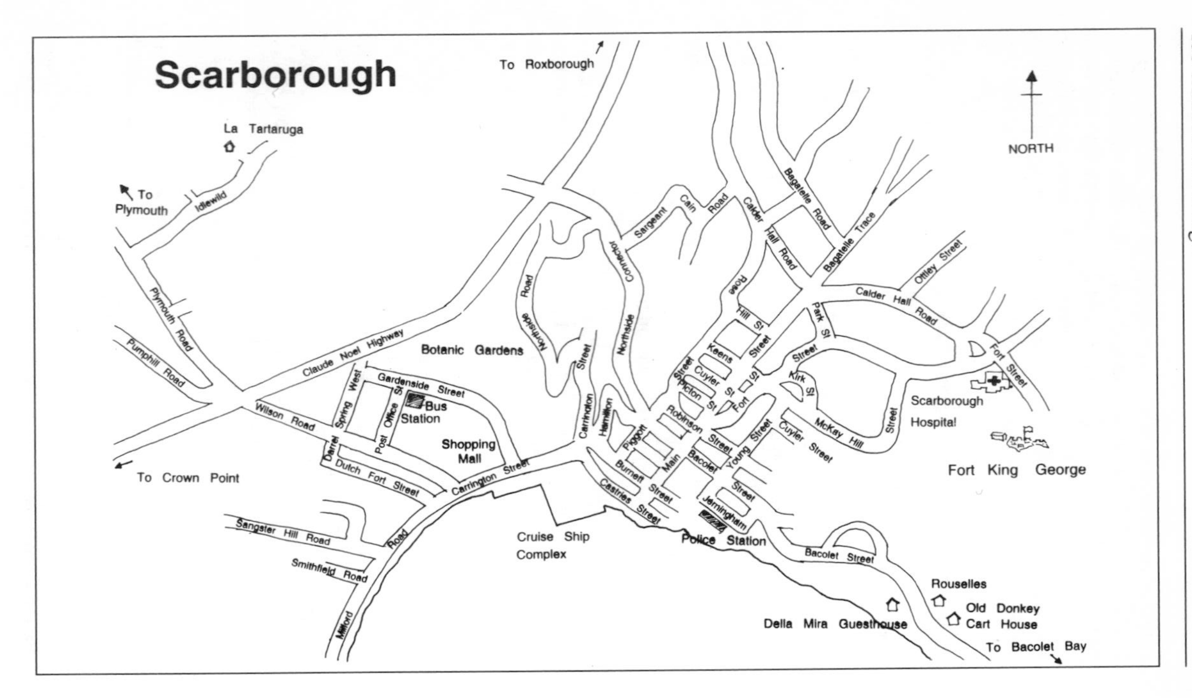

Scarborough
To Roxborough
NORTH
La Tartaruga
To Plymouth
Idlewild
Plymouth Road
Pumphill Road
Claude Noel Highway
Botanic Gardens
Gardenside Street
Bus Station
West
Spring
Post Office St
Wilson Road
Darrel
Dutch Fort Street
Shopping Mall
Carrington Street
To Crown Point
Sangster Hill Road
Smithfield Road
Road
Milford
Cruise Ship Complex
Northside Road
Connector
Northside
Street
Carrington
Hamilton
Sargeant
Cain Road
Calder Hall Road
Bagatelle Road
Bagatelle Trace
Ottley Street
Calder Hall Road
Rose
Hill St
Street
Keens
Cuyler St
Picton St
Fort St
Park St
Street
Kirk St
Piggott
Robinson Street
Main
Burnett Street
Castries Street
Bacolet
Young Street
Street
Jerningham
Police Station
Cuyler Street
McKay Hill Street
Fort Street
Scarborough Hospital
Fort King George
Bacolet Street
Rousselles
Old Donkey Cart House
Della Mira Guesthouse
To Bacolet Bay

containing five British and one French cannon.

Pigeon Point, lies north of Store Bay on a peninsular of land. One of the most photogenic places in the Caribbean, it fulfills the tropical dream: palm trees drooping lazily over an aquamarine ocean, a wooden jetty poking out to sea. A stunning place on a sunny day; only there is one snag, it is privately owned. The toll on the road is TT$ 10 or TT$ 5 for children, which you have to pay, though some enterprising locals enter along the beach for free.

Bon Accord Lagoon is a mangrove area and a popular habitat for birds, (for tours contact Adolphus James on 639 2231). Nearby is the ruin of a sugar plantation. The so-named Robinson Crusoe's Cave is near the airport but not particularly exciting. Further west is Canoe Bay, an area that is earmarked for future development.

Heading north up Shirvan Road you will pass the Starting Gate Pub on the right. Soon after on the left is the turning to Buccoo where the famous Sunday School event (see nightlife), is held. The beach here is muddy and disappointing. Another couple of kilometres north is **Mount Irvine**, the site of Tobago's only golf course, which is operated by the hotel of the same name.

Scarborough and the eastern coast

The Claude Noel Highway goes east from Crown Point Airport to the capital. It soon branches out into four lanes; this is the only stretch of major road on the island. The Highway avoids Scarborough so it is necessary to turn off to see the sights of the only town on Tobago.

The new **Cruise Ship Complex** is in the centre of town adjacent to where the ferry docks. Outside here, in a trough of sea water, is a huge seventeenth-century French cannon, which was dredged up when the terminal was being built. Around the harbour are the town's main public buildings: the Post Office, the market, the shopping mall, the library and the bus station. The Tobago Division of Tourism is based in the shopping mall.

Beside the town is the **Botanic Station and Gardens**, which can be reached by a path from the shopping mall. There is no admission fee to this well-kept area.

Piggott Street used to be the old marketplace till it was turned into St James' Park. Here stands a cenotaph honouring those who died in both World Wars. Opposite is the **Tobago House of Assembly**, which was built in 1925. Scarborough only became the capital in 1779 after Georgetown was abandoned.

Fort Street leads up to the hill with the most commanding view of the town. Along here is the Methodist Church built in 1824, the hopital which was begun in 1819 and the old town prison, where the grisly practice of hanging rebellious slaves was performed from the late 1700s.

Fort King George was built on the crown of the hill from 1777 till 1779. It was soon under attack, and in 1781 fell to the French who re-named it Fort Castries, before the British returned to repossess it in 1793. The views here are excellent, and the buildings have been well maintained by the Division of Tourism. The Fort consists of several old cannon, the powder magazine, the officer's mess, lighthouse and bell tower. One building has been converted into a tea room; another into an art gallery. Admission is free.

Heading out of town eastwards will mean crossing Gun Bridge, a single stone span bristling with cannon; this leads into the suburb of Bacolet. Here are a brace of good eating places; the **Old Donkey Cart** and **Rouselle's. Bacolet Bay** is where Walt Disney's *Swiss Family Robinson* was filmed. On the headland here is the shell of an old hotel, forlornly looking out to sea.

There are so many good bathing places on the drive eastwards, Hillsborough and Barbados Bays being just two of them. **Mount St George** opposite Barbados Bay was Tobago's first capital, this village contains the official residence of the Prime Minister. It was from here that the first sugar shipment was sent to Britain in 1770. The old court house of Georgetown has recently been refurbished as Studley Park House.

Fort Granby guards Barbados Bay. It still contains two old tombstones, one dating from 1772. Nearby is a great house named 'the Retreat'. Its owner must have had a sense of humour as this is where the British capitulated to the French in 1781.

There are two waterfalls in the vicinity. **Greenhill Waterfall** is five minutes from the road. **Goldsborough Waterfall** is slightly further and can be reached by walking up the shallow river bed. It is possible to swim in the pools here.

Further east is the **Richmond Great House**, a fine example of an eighteenth-century plantation house. It is owned by Professor Hollis Lynch, a Tobagonian who teaches at Columbia University. Inside the house is the finest collection of African art and sculpture in the country. Non-residents are welcome to dinner provided they make a reservation prior to arriving, (see above).

Plymouth and the western coast

From the **Mount Irvine Bay** right along the coast there are a series of beautiful bays. The most famous being **Turtle Beach** in **Great Courland Bay**. Here Giant Leatherbacks come each year to lay their

Mount Irvine Bay on Tobago's western coast. One of many fine beaches the island has to offer.

eggs. During the breeding season the Grafton, Mount Irvine and Turtle Beach Hotels put on lectures. The former hotel also runs a 'turtle watch'. At Black Rock is Fort Bennett, a small military sconce with a pair of cannon and fine views. The abandoned Grafton Estate is now a noted naturalist's site.

Great Courland Bay is named after the Courlanders who came from the Baltic seeking a new life. They were Protestants from the area now known as Latvia. The colonists had a hard time trying to establish a settlement here, repeated attempts were made from 1639 till 1693. Each failed; if the Amerindians did not defeat them, then the Dutch or the French would attack. Eventually the survivors merged into other settlements. The **Great Courland Bay Monument** in Plymouth is a tribute to them.

Plymouth is the main village on this coast. It prospered because of the large harbour beside it. A garrison was established here by the British in 1768, in the **Fort James**. When tested in action however, the soldiers failed to stop the French invasion fleet of 1781. The barracks and several old guns can still be seen.

The much-hyped **Mysterious Tombstone** is beside the main street. It became the resting place of Betty Stiven in 1783 and comes with an enigmatic inscription: 'She was a mother without knowing it and a wife without letting her husband know it except for her kind indulgences to him'. That is all we know about her. Plymouth is a pleasant place with a guesthouse, some rumshops, a snack bar and a charming wooden post office not much bigger than a telephone box.

Inland up the Courland River is the Craig Hill Falls. Further east is **Arnos Vale**; the hotel here is a former plantation house known for its garden, secluded bay and birdwatching. Beside the village is an old waterwheel which is now decaying through neglect.

As the windy road continues eastwards you pass through a few small fishing villages. The terrain gets more rugged and the road gets steadily worse, till shortly after Castara four-wheel drive vehicles are needed to get to Bloody Bay.

The north

Roxborough is the island's second settlement, and home of another small fort, the Louis D'Or Battery. Roxborough was the centre of the Belmanna Riots of 1876 caused by acute poverty, which eventually forced the planters to agree to a British colonial administration.

Near here are two waterfalls. The **Kings Bay Falls** used to be the best on the island, at over 30 metres high, but its water is now stored in a reservoir so its grandeur has been lost. Just outside Roxborough are the **Argyle Falls**. Turn off the Windward Road at the signpost, drive to the car park and make sure you secure your vehicle. Guides will meet you here and take you to the falls for TT$ 10 to TT$ 15 per person. It is about a 30-minute walk; the pools are large enough for swimming. Work is in progress on a snack bar and rest area nearby.

Moving northwards, **Speyside** is the next village, with a small guesthouse and a pleasant restaurant. The next bay along is **Blue Waters**, the home of the hotel of the same name and a base for some of the island's best diving. Beside the turn-off for this resort is a ruined plantation house and a rusting waterwheel.

This is a good place to go across to **Bird of Paradise Island**, also known as Little Tobago, and St Giles Island. **St Giles Island** is smaller and access is more difficult.

It was Sir William Ingram who in 1909 released a number of the Greater Bird of Paradise on Little Tobago. In 1928 the island was passed on to the government and is now managed by the Forestry Division. A total of 34 different species of bird can be seen by visitors to the island. The fees are TT$ 40 for one person, and TT$ 20 per person in larger groups, and this includes the boat trip. (The rates to visit St Giles Bird Sanctuary are $TT 75 for one person, $TT 60 per person in larger groups.)

The most northerly village is **Charlotteville**. Above this village is Flagstaff Hill and its lighthouse. Charlotteville sits on Man-of-War Bay, a fine natural harbour protected by the old guns of Fort Campbelton. Over the headland is the magnificent Pirate's Bay, which can be reached along a trail of over one hundred steps cut into the hillside.

The final route to be travelled to complete the tour of the island is from Roxborough to **Bloody Bay**, which was supposed to be the site of a fierce battle. Bloody Bay is an isolated village whose inhabitants make a living by seine fishing in the half-moon shaped bay. On the way you must pass the Main Ridge Recreation Site which is part of the Tobago Forest Reserve. This is the oldest protected land in the Western hemisphere, being decreed such in 1765. There is a vantage point on the top of the ridge and several hiking trails in the area of different lengths and complexity.

Excursions

For nature tours and hiking contact the following:
Mervyn Johnson (tel. 639 0576).

Pat's Nature Tours, Man-O-War Cottages, Charlotteville, (tel. 660 4327).
Mr David Rooks, Nature Tours, PO Box 348, Scarborough, (tel. 639 4276).
Ms Margaret Hinkson, Educatours, Carnbee, (tel. 639 7422).

For more general tours try the following agencies:
Ansyl Tours, (tel. 639 3865), offer one day tours to Trinidad or Grenada as well as fishing charters.
Hibiscus Tours, (tel. 638 2078), is a Trinidad-based company but has four organised tours of Tobago. The first is around Scarborough and Plymouth, the second Pigeon Point and Buccoo Reef, the third Buccoo Reef followed by a beach party and lastly a whole island tour.
Hospitality Services, (tel. 628 6552), are also Trinidad based. They have three tours; one a whole island day tour, another up to Charlotteville with stops at a waterfall on the way, and a third to the rainforest, hiking.
Sightseeing Tours, (tel. 628 1051). Trinidad based, they have excursions to Buccoo Reef, Charlotteville and one with a general itinery.
Tobago Travel Limited, telephone 639 8778 for details of their itineries.
Twin Island Tours, have an office at Milford Road near Crown Point Airport, (tel. 639 7491). Their trips can include the following itineries: Little Tobago, Speyside, the Rain Forest, Pigeon Point, Buccoo Reef, the Nylon Pool, Scarborough and the waterfalls.

For water colour enthusiasts **Jungle Art** (tel. 639 9405) run by Maureen Meyer, offer excursions. Anyone from amateurs to professionals is welcome. Alternatively Jungle Art can be contacted in the UK (tel. 081 950 1680) if a complete painting holiday is desired.

An excursion to Venezuela

A.J. Mauritzen offer one day to trips over to Venezuela which have been highly recommended. One is to Margarita for US$ 200. This includes transport to and from the hotel but not departure tax. The plane leaves at 0800 and returns to Tobago at 1930.

The same plane also continues to Angel Falls, with a stop for lunch in the Venezuelan rainforest. This costs US$ 275.

For reservations telephone 639 1092.

Annual events

January

This month sees a succession of pre-Carnival shows, in the form of indoor and outdoor calypso concerts.
Harvest, December and January are the harvest months, and a

number of agricultural festivals are held in January.
Horse racing on the Shirvan course.

February
Carnival usually falls within this month, occasionally, as in 1992, it falls in March. The main days are the Monday and Tuesday before Ash Wednesday. In the days beforehand there are an increasing number of concerts and parades. Though not on the scale of the Port of Spain celebrations Tobago Carnival is still an exciting and colourful event.

March/ April
Over Easter Tobago celebrates in some strange ways:
Crab racing is only similar to horse riding in that the aim is to cross the finishing line. No doubt the crabs are relieved that their jockeys do not ride them; instead they follow beside and try to prod their prodigies in the right way. Considering the crabs move sideways this is more difficult than it sounds. Who knows whether the winning or losing crab ends up in the pot?
Goat racing on the surface looks more like a proper race. The jockeys are tied to their large and sometimes bad-tempered sanaan goats. When the race begins the goats either refuse to budge or tear off in any direction, dragging their jockeys behind them to the howls of delight of a large crowd.

May
Game Fishing Classic a tournament of the International Game Fishing Association.

June
Tobago Open Golf is held at Mount Irvine on the 18-hole course.
St Peter's Day religious festival celebrates the fishing harvest at Charlotteville in a ceremony led by the Anglican Bishop. A range of seafood dishes are eaten at the feast.
Tourism Week is more of an internal promotion week for Tobagonians to understand the tourist business, but there are one or two events such as 'bum boat' racing.
Courlander's Week a celebration of the first settlers on the island. It includes a landing ceremony and art exhibition.

July/ August
Tobago Heritage Festival is aimed at preserving the island's culture. A range of competitions, parades and races are organised over most of the island.
Emancipation Day on 1 August begins with a race by power boats

from Trinidad to Store Bay. It is followed by shows and lectures.
St Peter's Day – this celebration is held in Castara, coming later than the others.
Independence Day on 31 August is a day of marches.

October
Natural History Festival promotes awareness of the environment through films, talks and hikes.

November
Prime Minister's Best Village Competition is a country-wide talent show of singing and dancing, which is battled out here as well as on Trinidad.

December
Christmas is celebrated a little differently to outside the Caribbean. It is a time of special foods and music.

Beaches

Tobago has no shortage of great bathing areas, most of which have been covered in the Sights section. A summary of the attractions of the main ones follows.

Pigeon Point is the most breathtaking beach on the island and has beach facilities, snack bars and a volleyball court. As it is a private beach some people come here unofficially for topless sunbathing. The snag is you are supposed to pay TT$ 10. For more information contact Pigeon Point Resorts Limited, PO Box 154, Tobago, (tel. 639 8141).
Store Bay is probably the most popular beach. It is quite small but is near all the amenities and hotels of the Crown Point area. The boats for Buccoo Reef and the Nylon Pool leave from here.
Canoe Bay is probably going to be developed in the near future; at the time of writing it was quiet.
Buccoo Bay is a bit of an eyesore; the island has a lot better to offer.
Mount Irvine Bay, **Stone Haven**, **Courland Bay** the sites, respectively, of the Mount Irvine Bay, Grafton and Turtle Beach Hotels. All are picturesque long beaches facing west.
Blue Waters Bay is a deep, sheltered beach in the north of the island which is the base of the best known diving operation.

The beaches mentioned above are those most developed for tourism. By driving north of Plymouth or east from Scarborough it is not difficult to find a secluded bay far away from the crowds. Perhaps the most impressive is **Pirate's Bay** near Charlotteville.

Sports

Birdwatching

This is excellent, given places like St Giles and Bird of Paradise islands. See the tours sections for guides.

Fishing

To hire boats contact either Mr Stanley Dillon, Buccoo, (tel. 639 8765), Ansyl Tours, (tel. 639 3865), or Mr Bob Wagner of Paradise Sea Sports, Speyside, (tel. 660 5206). See also the Trinidad Sports section for the address of the country's game fishing association who can be contacted for advice.

Golf

Tobago has the 18-hole **Mount Irvine Bay Golf Club**, Mount Irvine, Tobago, (tel. 639 8871). The yardage is 6,793 par 72. The USGAR is 72.3 for professionals, 71.9 for amateurs, 73.9 for ladies. The course, designed by Commander John Harris, is of international championship standard. It covers 150 acres of land and is equipped with an underground sprinkler system. The elevated tees ensure all hazards can be seen.

Guests are automatic members for the length of their stay with rates of TT$ 64 for nine holes, TT$ 128 for 18 holes. Non-residents are welcome but pay a higher levy; TT$ 72 for nine holes and TT$ 145 for 18 holes. Clubs can be hired for TT$ 34 for nine holes and TT$ 64 for 18 holes, carts for TT$ 64 for nine holes and TT$ 119 for 18 holes. VAT of 15% should be added to these prices.

Health club

There is a gymnasium with a mixture of fixed and free weights at the Grafton Beach Resort, (tel. 639 0191).

Horse riding

There are two stables on Tobago. One is based at the **Palm Tree Village Beach Resort**, Lambeau, (tel. 639 4347/9). One day's advance notice is requested. The stables are open through the week; everything is provided.

One of the most strikingly beautiful stretches of beachfront in the world, Pigeon Point has attracted the lenses of the professional photographer for years.

The **Park Stables**, Park Street, Scarborough, (tel. 639 2154), are located near Fort George. Rides are for the experienced, by appointment only.

Jogging

There are no laid out tracks on the island but some great views to run past.

Scuba

The island is highly rated as a diving location. It has some spectacular reefs off the north coast, such as the Charlotteville Alcyonarian Reef, which is a formation unique to the Caribbean, or the reefs around Speyside. This habitat attracts parrot fish, angel fish, sea whips, molluscs, fans, sea eggs, sea anenomes and sponges. Larger species include barracuda, manta rays, grouper, snapper and porpoises.

Sights that make Tobago exceptional include rare trigger fish and big tarpon, or Manta City off the coast of Little Tobago. The Black Forest at 120 feet has black coral formations over eight feet long.

Black Jack Hole off Little Tobago is a pleasant sloping reef dive; nearby is Japanese Gardens, on the edge of Goat Island. Here there are soft corals and variously shaped and coloured sponges. The London Bridge is through a winding chasm, coated in a range of corals and sponges.

The water clarity is at its best from December to May, at up to 120 feet. During the summer this drops to around 60 feet and begins to improve around October. From April till June there are large numbers of manta ray around Tobago's coast. The hyperbaric chambers for decompression are in Trinidad.

Derek Chung's **Tobago Dive Experience**, is the best sited operation to take advantage of the superb locations around the northern coast. Tobago Dive Experience are based at the Blue Waters Inn, Batteaux Bay, Speyside, (tel. 639 8781), with a concession at the Grafton Beach Resort.

Both PADI and NAUI certification is available, from beginners to full instructor level. A lot of the dives are very close at hand so travel time is kept to a minimum. Night and drift dives are possible and the operation maintains high safety standards. For diving rates contact Tobago Dive Experience directly.

Ken Young's **Dive Tobago**, (tel. 639 3695), offers a selection of coral and night dives. Their basic resort course costs US$ 50. The prices of the dives depend on whether they are with or without equipment. Without equipment the cost is US$ 30 for one dive, US$ 75 for three or US$ 110 for five. If equipment is needed this rises to US$ 35 for one dive, US$ 95 for three or US$ 140 for five.

John Darwent's **Tobago Marine Sports**, is at Store Bay, (tel. 639 0291). This programme includes night and reef dives. Without equipment rental the charges are TT$ 129 (US$ 30), for one dive, TT$ 365 (US$ 85) for three, TT$ 602 (US$ 140) for five dives. If equipment is necessary this will rise to (US$ 35) for one, US$ 95 for three or US$ 160 for five dives. There are other packages available, six day dives and a night dive cost US$ 200, ten day dives and one night dive cost US$ 275.

Snorkelling

There are many potential sites, most beaches have a wealth of interesting underwater life just off shore. This is in addition to the famous locations such as Buccoo Reef. Many hotels have snorkelling equipment their guests can hire, if not the rental stalls near the more popular beaches will have.

Squash

Grafton Beach Resort (Grafton, tel. 639 0191) has two newly-constructed courts. These are the only ones on the island.

Surfing

This is excellent in winter in the Mount Irvine Bay area. For more details contact the Surfing Association of Trinidad and Tobago, (tel. 637 0763).

Tennis

There are courts at Arnos Vale (tel. 639 2881/2), Blue Waters (tel. 660 4341), Crown Point Beach Hotel (tel. 639 8781/3), Grafton Beach Resort (tel. 639 0191), Turtle Beach Hotel (tel. 639 2851) and the Mount Irvine Bay (tel. 639 8871). Typical rates are TT$ 10 per hour for guests, TT$ 20 for non-residents; there is often a surcharge for night-play.

Walking

For the best trails contact the tourist offices. There is plenty to choose from and they will be best placed to recommend guides or routes.

Windsurfing and watersports

Jetskis have appeared off the Store Bay area but there are no places that offer parasailing at present. The larger resorts will have windsurfers available. Waterskiing can be arranged at Tobago Marine Sports Ltd, Store Bay (tel. 639 0291). A number of stalls are springing up in this area with equipment for hire.

Grafton Beach Resort (tel. 639 0191) and the Turtle Beach Resort (tel. 639 2851/2), have their own watersports programme.

Shopping

Scarborough is the only town of any size on Tobago though shopping is not only limited to here. There are some small boutiques and shops scattered around the island. Opening hours can vary considerably but are typically from 0800 till 1600 or 1630, from Monday to Thursday. Saturdays vary; it can be from 0800 till 1200 or through the afternoon. Sunday closing is strictly observed.

Some places of interest include:

Cotton House (Bacolet Road), adjacent to the Old Donkey Cart. The shop has a large range of batik garments and fabrics.

Island Concepts (Jermingham Street, Scarborough, tel. 639 5058), has a good selection of clothes and handicrafts.

Nairobi (Shirvan Road), is a small boutique located beside the Starting Gate Pub.

Scarborough Mall, the town's largest development in recent years. This is where you will find the largest variety of shops gathered in one place. Many are especially geared to visitors' needs, selling a range of fashions, books, prints or other kinds of souvenirs.

Vendors Mall is a collection of market stalls. These sell a range of craftwork, clothes and pirate cassette tapes. Many of the clothes are flown over duty free from Margarita in Venezuela. The quoted price is often not the final price if you put up a struggle and have a go at bargaining.

Most of the larger hotels have concessionary shops on site. In a small pace like Tobago they often stock a fair selection of the goods available. If you despair of finding what you desire, remember that most Tobagonians go to Port of Spain to shop when they can.

Turtle watching

Spotting the Leatherback Turtle is a seasonal event, with nesting taking place between March and August. The turtles can weigh up to 728 kilograms and have a carapace of up to 185 cm long. Their favourite area is between Mount Irvine and Plymouth.

Nesting is best observed between 1900 and 0500. The female makes her way up the beach and excavates a hole with her flippers then lays between 80 and 125 eggs. After an incubation of 55 to 70 days the baby turtles emerge and make a dash for the ocean. This is one of nature's most epic struggles; only the tiniest fraction of hatchlings will ever return here. The body count will reach 40% before the babies reach the relative safety of the ocean.

Certain rules should be observed by turtle watchers. No loud noises should be made, nor any lights brighter than a flashlight used. Absolute silence should be observed till turtles have dug their nest sites. Only while they are laying their eggs should they be photographed. Do not disturb them on their return to the sea and do not handle the eggs after they have left.

The Grafton Beach Resort has a Turtle Watch Club to help protect this fascinating species.

Appendix
Wind Force: The Beaufort Scale*

B'Fort No.	Wind Descrip.	Effect on land	Effect on sea	Wind Speed knots	mph	kph	Wave height (m)†
0	Calm	Smoke rises vertically	Sea like a mirror		less than 1		-
1	Light air	Direction shown by smoke but not by wind vane	Ripples with appearance of scales; no foam crests	1-3	1-3	1-2	-
2	Light breeze	Wind felt on face; leaves rustle; wind vanes move	Small wavelets; crests do not break	4-6	4-7	6-11	0.15-0.30
3	Gentle breeze	Leaves and twigs in motion wind extends light flag	Large wavelets; crests begin to break; scattered white horses	7-10	8-12	13-19	0.60-1.00
4	Moderate breeze	Small branches move; dust and loose paper raised	Small waves becoming longer; fairly frequent white horses	11-16	13-18	21-29	1.00-1.50
5	Fresh breeze	Small trees in leaf begin to sway	Moderate waves; many white horses; chance of some spray	17-21	19-24	30-38	1.80-2.50
6	Strong breeze	Large branches in motion; telegraph wires whistle	Large waves begin to form; white crests extensive; some spray	22-27	25-31	40-50	3.00-4.00

7	Near gale	Whole trees in motion; difficult to walk against wind	Sea heaps up; white foam from breaking waves begins to be blown in streaks	28-33	32-38	51-61	4.00-6.00
8	Gale	Twigs break off trees; progress impeded	Moderately high waves; foam blown in well-marked streaks	34-40	39-46	62-74	5.50-7.50
9	Strong gale	Chimney pots and slates blown off	High waves; dense streaks of foam; wave crests begin to roll over; heavy spray	41-47	47-54	75-86	7.00-9.75
10	Storm	Trees uprooted; considerable structural damage	Very high waves, overhanging crests; dense white foam streaks; sea takes on white appearance; visibility affected	48-56	55-63	87-100	9.00-12.50
11	Violent storm	Widespread damage, seldom experienced in England	Exceptionally high waves; dense patches of foam; wave crests blown into froth; visibility affected	57-65	64-75	101-110	11.30-16.00
12	Hurricane	Winds of this force encountered only in the tropics	Air filled with foam & spray; visibility seriously affected	65+	75+	110+	13.70+

* Introduced in 1805 by Sir Francis Beaufort (1774-1857), hydrographer to the Navy.
† First figure indicates average height of waves; second figure indicates maximum height.

INDEX